101 Great
Answers
to the Toughest
Interview
Questions

2nd Edition

By
Ron Fry

101 Great Answers to the Toughest Interview Questions

2nd Edition

By
Ron Fry

CAREER PRESS
180 Fifth Avenue
P.O. Box 34
Hawthorne, NJ 07507
1-800-CAREER-1
201-427-0229 (outside U.S.)
FAX: 201-427-2037

101 GREAT ANSWERS TO THE TOUGHEST INTERVIEW QUESTIONS (2ND EDITION) ISBN 1-56414-119-5, $8.95
Cover design byThe Gottry Communications Group, Inc.
Printed in the U.S.A. by Book-mart Press

To order this title by mail, please include price as noted above, $2.50 handling per order, and $1.00 for each book ordered. Send to: Career Press, Inc., 180 Fifth Ave., P.O. Box 34, Hawthorne, NJ 07507

Or call toll-free 1-800-CAREER-1 (Canada: 201-427-0229) to order using VISA or MasterCard, or for further information on books from Career Press.

Library of Congress Cataloging-in-Publication Data

Fry, Ron.
    101 great answers to the toughest interview questions / by Ron Fry. -- 2nd ed.
        p. cm.
    Includes index.
    ISBN 1-56414-119-5 : $8.95
    1. Employment interviewing. I. Title. II. Title: One hundred one great answers to the toughest interview questions. III. Title: One hundred and one great answers to the toughest interview questions.
HF5549.5.I6F75   1994
650.14--dc20   93-45846
                                                                    CIP

Dedication

To my daughter Lindsay, who has more questions than one father could ever answer. Hopefully, by the time she grows up, she'll find her own answers to all of them.

Contents

The Interrogation

I still break out in a cold sweat remembering it.

I had burned the midnight oil the night before my first job interview, preparing to knock 'em dead. First, I pored over old class notes to refresh myself on the basic skills I would need in order to perform the proofreading job I was applying for.

Confident of my expertise, I practiced waxing poetic about my previous work experience. Never mind that it was a part-time summer job in the local grocery store! It showed that I was responsible, versatile, resourceful—in other words, management material.

By this time, I knew my prospective employer would be dazzled. But I wanted to leave no doubt that I was the right man for the job. So I memorized 10 show-stopping questions about the company I hoped to join. By that time, I knew their bottom line better than my own and I was looking forward to showcasing the research I'd done.

Before I switched off the light to turn in that night, I remember seeing my image in my favorite rehearsal mirror—the picture of confidence. This was going to be *no sweat*.

And it started out that way.

When Mr. Hogan came out to the reception area to greet me, he looked like a pushover! My confidence rose four notches. In no time at all, I thought smugly, they'd be thanking their lucky stars for hiring me. And one day soon, by God, I'd have Hogan's job!

After taking a moment to study my resume and application, Mr. Hogan looked up at me and said, "So, tell me about yourself."

My mind went blank. What was he looking for?

I smiled nervously as I desperately tried to call forth some of the little speeches I had so diligently rehearsed. Meanwhile, I could feel my palms sweating profusely. I couldn't think of where to begin—so I rambled. Along the way, I sputtered an embarrassing number of "ah's" and "um's."

To make a long and excruciating story short, I didn't get that job. (Let alone Mr. Hogan's!) And I've often suspected that it was because I couldn't be more concise about telling him "a little about myself."

Practice Makes Perfect

Instead of giving up (which I admit I felt like doing after leaving Mr. Hogan's office that day), I decided to plunge into the interviewing process with even greater gusto. Fortunately—and only after a lot more interviews—I got better. Now as a veteran of the other side of the desk as well (I've hired more than 100 people and interviewed more than 1,000), I can tell you that interviewing is more serious business than ever before.

There are more good applicants. And fewer jobs. Employers are looking for "self-managing" employees—

people who are versatile, confident and not afraid to roll up their sleeves and get the job done. But you can't get started proving yourself without making it through the interview process.

Let's face it. Interviewing was never easy. But of all the tools in your professional arsenal, your ability to shine in that brief moment in time—your initial interview—can make or break your chances for a second, and ultimately a shot at the job.

Like playing the piano, interviewing takes practice. And practice makes perfect. The hours of personal interviewing experience—the tragedies and the triumphs—as well as years as an interviewer are the basis for this book. It is the book I wish I'd studied the night before facing the Grand Inquisitor Hogan. My intention is to spare you many of the indignities I suffered along the way by helping you prepare for the interview of your worst nightmares—at a comfortable distance from the interviewer's glare.

After my dubious beginning, there came a time when I even started anticipating job interviews with some sort of perverse enthusiasm. Let them try to stump me this time!

Will you have to answer all 101 questions included here? Certainly not. (At least not in one interview.) But chances are better than average that the questions tomorrow's interviewer doesn't ask will be on the tip of the next interviewer's tongue. That's the way it works.

Think on Your Feet

Most interviewers are not trying to torture you for sport. They use tough questions to get right to the heart of specific issues. Their motive is to quickly gain knowledge about you that will help them make a decision. By the same token, when you know what they're looking for, you can prepare to give them the information they seek. (And reduce your own fear and anxiety at the same time.)

So beginning with that open-ended killer—"Tell me a little about yourself" (my personal favorite), I've grouped all the questions I've fielded by chapter. All 101 are listed in Chapter 16.

Is this the ultimate crib sheet? Sort of. But I hope you'll take it a step further and use these questions as the basis for some thoughtful self-exploration. You'll need to be prepared to think for yourself—on your feet, not by the seat of your pants.

How to Use This Book

After an introduction to the process of interviewing in Chapters 1 and 2, I'll ask you to begin writing down your answers to the questions presented, using my advice and examples as a guideline.

I urge you to spend time refining these answers. Polish them until they glitter. Read them over and over again so you become familiar and comfortable with them. Take time to memorize some (Don't worry, I'll tell you which ones.) so you can repeat them verbatim to the interviewer in a way that sounds spontaneous and enthusiastic—not tired and rehearsed.

A lot of work, you say? It might sound like a daunting challenge right now. But I assure you, by the time you finish this book, you'll actually be looking forward to the challenge of your next job interview.

So, good luck. And try to keep those palms dry!

Chapter 1

Why You Can't Just "Wing It"

Think of the last salesperson who really sold you. Not the pushy guy who tried so hard to pressure you into buying that you were tempted to say yes, just so he'd shut up.

Think of the last person who made you want to buy. How did he or she do it? Probably not by using hard-sell tactics or a slick spiel. Instead this person probably took the time to understand your needs and explain how each feature of the product you were considering would meet those needs. No doubt, you still remember this individual not for taking your money, but for doing you a favor.

The Product is *You*

The interviewing process is also a kind of sale. In this case, you are the product—and the salesperson. If you show up unprepared to talk about your unique features and benefits, you're not likely to motivate an interviewer to "buy."

Too many candidates hesitate, then stump and stutter their way through a disjointed litany of resume "bites." Other interviewees recite canned replies that only demonstrate a skill for memorizing to the experienced interviewer.

The sad fact is that too many job candidates are unprepared to talk about themselves. You may have filed a gorgeous resume and cover letter. You may be wearing the perfect clothes on the day of the interview. But if you can't convince the interviewer—face-to-face—that you are the right person for the job, you aren't likely to make the sale.

The object of this chapter is to get you ready to comfortably answer one—and only one—question: "Who are you?" The entire interview will hinge on how well you know—and can speak about—this one topic.

I'm assuming that, like most people, you are a complex product—made up of a unique blend of abilities, skills and personal qualities and shaped by your own personal and professional history. Believe me, the time you spend outlining the detail of your own life will pay off in interviews, and ultimately job offers. This chapter will guide you through the process.

What You Should Know About You

You already know your life by heart—after all, you've been living it for the last few decades, right? But you'll be amazed to see how much detail you can remember (and ultimately how it will fit together in the context of your next career move) once you write it down.

So, your first step is to build a complete dossier on yourself. The eight Data Input Sheets at the end of this chapter will help you organize all kinds of information about yourself. With this information in place, it will be easier to develop concise and convincing answers to almost any interview questions—answers that will set you apart from the competition.

Here's a brief look at the various Data Input Sheets.

Employment Data Input Sheet

Prepare a separate sheet for every full-time and part-time job you've ever held, no matter how short the tenure. Yes, even summer jobs are important here. They demonstrate resourcefulness, responsibility and initiative—that you were already developing a sense of independence while you were still living at home.

For each employer, include:

- Name, address and telephone number.
- The names of all of your supervisors and, whenever possible, where they can be reached.
- Letter of recommendation, if they cannot be reached.
- The exact dates (month and year) you were employed.

For each job, include:

- Your specific duties and responsibilities, such as "financial responsibilities" and "purchasing authority."
- Supervisory experience, noting the number of people you supervised.
- Specific skills required for the job.

- Your key accomplishments.
- The dates you received promotions.
- Any awards, honors and special recognition you received.

For each part-time job, include:

- The number of hours you worked per week.

Don't write a *book* on each job. But do concentrate on providing *specific data* (volume of work handled, problems solved, dollars saved) to provide an objective measurement of your abilities and accomplishments. Believe me, these hard facts will add a powerful punch to your interview presentation. For example:

Duties. Write one or two sentences giving an overview of the tasks you handled in each of the jobs you held. Use numbers as much as possible to demonstrate the scope of your responsibilities. For example, an experienced salesperson might write:

- Responsible for managing 120 active accounts in sales territory that contributed $3 million in annual revenues.
- Reviewed activity of three telephone salespeople.

Skills. Name the specific abilities you had to have to perform your duties—highlighting those that you developed on the job. The same salesperson might write:

- Trained other sales staff in new product lines.
- Handled telephone support for customer base of 100.

Key accomplishments. This is the place to "brag." But be sure to back up each accomplishment with specifics, including results. For example:

- Developed new call-reporting system that increased volume in territory 20 percent within 18 months.

- Oversaw computerization of department that helped realize cost savings of 15 percent.

Volunteer Work Data Input Sheet

Having hired more than 100 people during my career, I can attest to the fact that your "after-hours" activities can mean a lot to employers. Workaholics rarely make best employees.

So take some time to make a detailed record of your volunteer pursuits, similar to the one you've just completed for each job you've held.

For each volunteer organization, include:

- Name, address and telephone number.
- The name of your supervisor or the director of the organization.
- Letter of recommendation.
- The exact dates (month and year) of your involvement with the organization.

For each volunteer experience, include:

- The approximate number of hours you devoted to the activity each month.
- Your specific duties and responsibilities.

- Specific skills required.
- Accomplishments.
- Any awards, honors and special recognition you received.

Educational Data Input Sheets

If you're a recent college graduate or still in college, you don't need to rehash your high school experiences. If you have a graduate degree or are a graduate student, however, you should list details on both graduate and undergraduate course work. If you're still in school and graduation is more than a year away, indicate the number of credits you've already earned through the most recent semester completed.

Activities Data Input Sheet

I'm always interested in—and impressed by—candidates who talk about books they've read and activities they enjoy. So make a list of all the sports, clubs and other activities in which you've participated, inside or outside of school.

For each activity, club or group, include:

- The name and purpose.
- Any offices you held, special committees you formed, chaired or participated on or specific positions you played.
- The duties and responsibilities of each role.
- Key accomplishments.
- Any awards or honors you received.

Awards and Honors Data Input Sheet

List all the awards and honors you've received from school(s), community groups, church groups, clubs, and so on. You may include awards from prestigious high schools (prep schools or professional schools) even if you're in graduate school or long out of college.

Military Service Data Input Sheet

Many employers are impressed by the maturity of candidates who have served in the armed forces. Some may consider military service excellent management training for many civilian jobs. So if you've served in the armed forces, even for a short time, make sure you can discuss your experiences and how it would be pertinent to your professional aspirations.

For each experience, include:

- Final rank awarded.
- Duties and responsibilities.
- Citations and awards.
- Details on specific training and/or any special schooling.
- Special skills developed.
- Key accomplishments.

Language Data Input Sheet

Even if you're not applying for a job in the international arena, your ability to read, write and speak a second language can make you invaluable to employers in an increasing number of multinational companies. One year of college Russian won't cut it. But if you spent a year studying in Moscow—and can carry on a conversation with a native—by all means write it down.

Putting it in *Your* Perspective

Once you've finished completing these forms, you'll have a lot of information—facts—about what you've done and where.

But any interviewer worth his or her stuff will be looking for more. So once you've finished with the fact-finding, practice putting it all in perspective. Your unique, personal perspective, that is. Write down your answers to the following questions that you can expect an interviewer to be interested in asking:

1. Which achievements did you enjoy most? Which are you proudest of? (Be ready to tell the interviewer how these accomplishments can add to the position at hand.)
2. What mistakes have you made? Why did they occur? How have you learned from them and what have you done to keep similar things from occurring again?
3. How well do you interact with authority figures—such as bosses, teachers, parents?

Now, Put Yourself on the Hot Seat

It's time to get to know yourself just a little better. So pull out a sheet of fresh paper and tackle some more tough questions. Remember, your answers will be for your eyes only. So swallow hard, and be honest.

1. What are your favorite games and sports? Think about the way you play these games

and what that says about you. Are you overly competitive? Do you give up too easily? Are you a good loser—or a bad winner? Do you rise to a challenge, or back away from it?

2. What kinds of people are your friends? Do you associate only with people who are very similar to you? Do you enjoy differences in others—or merely tolerate them? What are some things that have caused you to end friendships? What does this say about you?

3. If you were to ask a group of friends and acquaintances to describe you, what adjectives would they use? List all of them—the good and the bad. Why would people describe you in this way? Are there specific behaviors, skills, achievements or failures that seem to identify you in the eyes of others? What are they?

What's the Point?

By now, you're probably a bit uncomfortable—and wondering, "What's the point of all this soul-searching? After all, I'm just trying to get ready for a job interview!"

The point is this: The better you know yourself, the better you can sell yourself to a prospective employer when you're on the spot in an interview.

If you've ever taken a course in marketing, you know that the best way to sell a product is to describe its best features, as well as the benefits of each of those features. But if you aren't also prepared to answer objections about the product's weaker points, you won't be in a strong position to convince a savvy buyer to buy.

101 Interview Questions

From your Data Input Sheets, you can compile a list of your best features under the following headings:

- My strongest skills.
- My greatest areas of knowledge.
- My greatest personality strengths.
- The things I do best.
- My key accomplishments.

Now transform your best features into benefits for your prospective company.

1. What in my personal inventory will convince this employer that I deserve the position?
2. What are the strengths, achievements, skills and areas of knowledge that make me most qualified for this position? What in my background should separate me from the herd of other applicants?

By answering some tough questions about the mistakes you've made—and the less-than-positive feedback you've gotten—you can also locate areas that may need improvement. Do you need to develop new skills? Improve you relations with those in authority? If you have been thorough and brutally honest (and it may feel brutal!), you may find out things about yourself that you never knew, Or, more accurately, that you never *knew* you knew. So also write down:

- Which of my weaknesses should I admit to when asked? How will I explain the ways I've improved?

Getting Comfortable on the Hot Seat

If you're still not convinced about the value of putting in this much work, read on. Even a passing glance at the questions in the chapters ahead should indicate gaps in your own answers to some of them if you try to "wing it."

The more effort you spend filling in those gaps now—with a cool head—the less you'll sweat once you're in the interviewer's hot seat. It's up to you.

But before we forge ahead to the first of the questions you're likely to field, let's take a closer look at the interview process itself, in Chapter 2.

EMPLOYMENT DATA INPUT SHEET

Employer Name: _____

Address: _____

Address: _____

Phone: _____

Dates of Employment: _____ to _____

Hours Per Week: _____ Salary/Pay: _____

Supervisor's Name & Title: _____

Duties: _____

_____

_____

Skills Utilized: _____

_____

_____

Accomplishments/Honors/Awards: _____

_____

_____

Other Important Information: _____

_____

EMPLOYMENT DATA INPUT SHEET

Employer Name: _____

Address: _____

Address: _____

Phone: _____

Dates of Employment: _____ to _____

Hours Per Week: _____ Salary/Pay: _____

Supervisor's Name & Title: _____

Duties: _____

_____

_____

Skills Utilized: _____

_____

_____

Accomplishments/Honors/Awards: _____

_____

_____

Other Important Information: _____

_____

_____

EMPLOYMENT DATA INPUT SHEET

Employer Name: _____

Address: _____

Address: _____

Phone: _____

Dates of Employment: _____ to _____

Hours Per Week: _____ Salary/Pay: _____

Supervisor's Name & Title: _____

Duties: _____

_____

_____

Skills Utilized: _____

_____

_____

Accomplishments/Honors/Awards: _____

_____

_____

Other Important Information: _____

_____

_____

EMPLOYMENT DATA INPUT SHEET

Employer Name: _____

Address: _____

Address: _____

Phone: _____

Dates of Employment: _____ to _____

Hours Per Week: _____ Salary/Pay: _____

Supervisor's Name & Title: _____

Duties: _____

_____

_____

Skills Utilized: _____

_____

_____

Accomplishments/Honors/Awards: _____

_____

_____

Other Important Information: _____

_____

VOLUNTEER WORK DATA INPUT SHEET

Organization Name: _____

Address: _____

Address: _____

Phone: _____   Hours Per Week: _____

Dates of Activity: _____

Supervisor's Name & Title: _____

Duties: _____

_____

_____

Skills Utilized: _____

_____

_____

Accomplishments/Honors/Awards: _____

_____

_____

Other Important Information: _____

_____

_____

_____

VOLUNTEER WORK DATA INPUT SHEET

Organization Name:_____

Address:_____

Address:_____

Phone:_____   Hours Per Week:_____

Dates of Activity:_____

Supervisor's Name & Title:_____

Duties:_____

_____

_____

Skills Utilized:_____

_____

_____

Accomplishments/Honors/Awards:_____

_____

_____

Other Important Information:_____

_____

_____

_____

101 Interview Questions

HIGH SCHOOL DATA INPUT SHEET

School Name:_____

Address:_____

Address:_____

Phone:_____   Years Attended:_____

Major Studies:_____

GPA/Class Rank:_____

Honors:_____

Important Courses:_____

OTHER SCHOOL DATA INPUT SHEET

School Name:_____

Address:_____

Address:_____

Phone:_____   Years Attended:_____

Major Studies:_____

GPA/Class Rank:_____

Honors:_____

Important Courses:_____

COLLEGE DATA INPUT SHEET

College: _____

Address: _____

Phone: _____ Years Attended: _____

Degrees Earned: _____ Major: _____

Minor: _____ Honors: _____

_____

Important Courses: _____

_____

_____

GRADUATE SCHOOL DATA INPUT SHEET

College: _____

Address: _____

Phone: _____ Years Attended: _____

Degrees Earned: _____ Major: _____

Minor: _____ Honors: _____

_____

Important Courses: _____

ACTIVITIES DATA INPUT SHEET

Club/Activity: _____

Office(s) Held: _____

Description of Participation: _____

_____

Duties/Responsibilities: _____

_____

_____

Club/Activity: _____

Office(s) Held: _____

Description of Participation: _____

_____

Duties/Responsibilities: _____

_____

_____

Club/Activity: _____

Office(s) Held: _____

Description of Participation: _____

_____

Duties/Responsibilities: _____

_____

ACTIVITIES DATA INPUT SHEET

Club/Activity: _____

Office(s) Held: _____

Description of Participation: _____

_____

Duties/Responsibilities: _____

_____

_____

Club/Activity: _____

Office(s) Held: _____

Description of Participation: _____

_____

Duties/Responsibilities: _____

_____

_____

Club/Activity: _____

Office(s) Held: _____

Description of Participation: _____

_____

Duties/Responsibilities: _____

_____

AWARDS & HONORS DATA INPUT SHEET

Name of Award, Citation, Etc.: _____

From Whom Received: _____

Date: _____ Significance: _____

_____

Other Pertinent Information: _____

_____

_____

Name of Award, Citation, Etc.: _____

From Whom Received: _____

Date: _____ Significance: _____

_____

Other Pertinent Information: _____

_____

_____

Name of Award, Citation, Etc.: _____

From Whom Received: _____

Date: _____ Significance: _____

_____

Other Pertinent Information: _____

_____

MILITARY SERVICE DATA INPUT SHEET

Branch: _____

Rank (at Discharge): _____

Dates of Service: _____

Duties & Responsibilities: _____

_____

_____

_____

Special Training and/or School Attended: _____

_____

_____

_____

_____

Citations, Awards, etc.: _____

_____

_____

Specific Accomplishments: _____

_____

_____

LANGUAGE DATA INPUT SHEET

Language:_____

☐ Read   ☐ Write   ☐ Converse

Background (number of years studied, travel, etc.): _____

_____

_____

_____

Language:_____

☐ Read   ☐ Write   ☐ Converse

Background (number of years studied, travel, etc.): _____

_____

_____

_____

Language:_____

☐ Read   ☐ Write   ☐ Converse

Background (number of years studied, travel, etc.): _____

_____

_____

_____

Chapter 2

What You're Up Against

The days of filling out the standard application and chatting your way through one or two interviews are gone. These days, interviewers and hiring managers are reluctant to leave anything to chance. Many have begun to experiment with the latest techniques for data-gathering and analysis. For employers, interviewing has gone from an art to a full-fledged science.

Does this make you feel like a specimen under a microscope? Get used to it. Times are tougher for companies, so it's natural to assume that interviews will be tougher for their prospective employees.

In the many years I've subscribed to human resources journals, I've noticed an increasing number of new interviewing methods developed to help interviewers measure, as accurately as possible, how well prospective candidates would perform on the job. The "database interview," the "situational interview," and the "stress (confrontational) interview" are only a few of the special treatments you might encounter on your way to landing the ideal job.

The good news is that companies hoping to survive in our new service economy will depend on the human element—you—as their most valuable business asset. But because there are more "humans" competing for fewer jobs, employers will be focused on hiring only the very best applicants.

Interviewing has always been a challenge. But these days it is serious business. Consider:

The incredible shrinking company. Rampant downsizing has left fewer jobs. At the same time, the "cost of hire"—the amount of money it takes to land a suitable candidate for a job—has escalated dramatically in recent years.

From business suit to lawsuit. Lawsuits against employers for wrongful discharge and other employment-related causes have also increased exponentially over the past decade. Hiring mistakes can be costly, making it more important than ever for companies to be sure the people they do hire will be right for the job.

The great cattle call. Although the labor force is indeed shrinking as a result of the much ballyhooed "baby bust," you're liable to face a new kind of competition as a job applicant. These days, you can expect to bump into fellow candidates at every level of experience on the way to or from your first interview—or your fourth.

Where Does That Leave You?

More employers seem to be looking for a special kind of employee—someone with experience, confidence and the initiative to learn what he or she needs to know. Someone who requires very little supervision. Someone with a hands-on attitude—from beginning to end.

Since it's difficult to tell all that from an application and handshake, here's what's happening:

Passing the test(s). You'll probably have to go through more interviews than your predecessors for the same job—no matter what your level of expertise. Knowledge and experience still give you an inside edge. But these days, you'll need stamina, too. Your honesty, your intelligence, your mental health—even the toxicity of your blood—may be measured before you can be considered fully assessed.

Braving more interviews. You may also have to tiptoe through a mine field of different types of interview situations—and keep your head—to survive as a new hire.

Don't go out and subscribe to a human resources journal. Just do all you can to remain confident and flexible—and ready with your answers. No matter what kind of interview you find yourself in, this approach should carry you through with flying colors.

Let's take a brief no-consequences tour of the interview circuit.

Level One: The Screening Interview

If you're pursuing a job at a mid-size or large company (any organization of more than 250 employees), your first interview is likely to begin in the human resources department.

101 Interview Questions

What can you expect? Let's say you're applying for your dream job as a middle manager at ABC Widget Co. Arriving on time for your first interview, you're greeted by Heather.

Heather is a lower-level person in the human resources department. She's been given a bare-bones introduction to the duties and responsibilities you must have to operate successfully in the position you're after. If she's not completely up to speed, it's probably not her fault. The person who will manage this new position (the hiring manager) may not have had time to fill out a detailed position description, or to tell Heather exactly what he or she is looking for.

Regardless of how much she's got to go on, Heather's job is pretty simple: weed out the number of candidates whose resumes jibe with the short version of the job description, so that the hiring manager will have fewer candidates to interview.

After you've gotten through the preliminaries, Heather is likely to follow a script. She will ask questions to see if you have the qualifications for the position: the appropriate degree, the right amount of experience, a willingness to relocate, and so on.

Heather will be trying to determine whether you've been completely truthful on your resume. Did you work where and when you claim? Have the titles and responsibilities you're bragging about? Make the salaries you've stated?

The screening interview may also drift into a few qualitative areas. Does she think you're sufficiently enthusiastic? Do you sound intelligent? Exhibit any obvious emotional disturbances? Are you articulate? Energetic? Are you the type of person who would fit well within the department, and the company?

Getting Past the Gate

If you pass the screening hurdle, Heather may resort to an arsenal of professional interviewing techniques. Remember, Heather is trained and practiced in the science of interviewing.

While it's still up to the hiring manager to decide whether you'll still be checking the classified ads next week, Heather has the power, at this point, to keep you from meeting the hiring manager! She is, in effect, the gatekeeper.

But once you get past the gate, be careful of what's on the other side.

1. The Stress Interview

Anyone who's been through one of these never forgets it. The stress interview is designed to cut through the veneer of pleasantries to the heart of the matter. To see what a candidate is really made of.

I was subjected to a stress interview before I'd ever heard of the technique—not the best way to prepare, believe me.

Several years ago, I applied for an editorial position at a major publishing company. I made it past the first hurdle, a screening interview conducted in the corporate office. Next, I was invited to come back to meet the director of personnel, Carrie. After greeting me pleasantly, Carrie led me back to her rather palatial office. We chatted for a few minutes as I settled in. Then everything changed. Suddenly, I was undergoing an interrogation—worthy of the secret police in a country on Amnesty International's Top Ten.

Assuming that I had been given good reviews by the first screening interviewer, I was shocked when Carrie

41

began firing. First she questioned my credentials. Why, she wondered sarcastically, had I majored in liberal arts rather than something "practical." She demanded to know what in the world made me think that I could edit a magazine (even though I had been doing it quite well for years).

Each successive question skittered in a dizzying new direction. If the first question was about my work experience, the next launched into my fitness routine, and the next, my favorite movie.

Carrie's questions did exactly what I later discovered they were intended to do—they made me feel confused, fearful and hostile. I behaved badly, I admit. I answered most of her questions in monosyllables, avoiding her eyes.

Needless to say, I was not offered the job.

But I did learn some valuable lessons from Carrie that day:

- **Never let them see you sweat.** In other words, no matter how stressful the situation, stay calm. Never take your eyes from the interviewer. When he or she finishes asking a question, take a few seconds to compose yourself and then, and only then, answer.

- **Recognize the situation for what it is.** It is nothing more than an artificial scenario designed to see how you react under pressure. The interviewer probably has nothing against you personally.

- **Don't become despondent.** It's easy to think that the interviewer has taken a strong dislike to you and that your chances for completing the interview process are nil. That's not the case. The stress interview is designed to see if you will become depressed, hostile and flustered when the going gets tough.

- **Watch your tone of voice.** It's easy to become sarcastic during a stress interview, especially if you don't realize what the interviewer is up to.

2. The Situational Interview

"What would happen if everyone else called in sick and...?"

There's nothing quite like the terror of the hypothetical question. Especially when it is a product of the interviewer's rich imagination. We'll talk more about these devils in Chapter 9. But for now, know that the hypothetical question should start a red light flashing in your consciousness. It is your signal that you are about to undergo an increasingly popular type of interview—the situational interview.

The premise is sound. Present the candidate with situations that might, hypothetically, occur on the job in order to gauge the degree to which he or she demonstrates the traits that will lead to success.

But what's good for the interviewer is often deadly for the interviewee. You will have to devote a great deal of thought to each of these questions. If you find yourself caught in this snare, stay calm and use the homework you have already done on your personal inventory to untangle yourself.

3. The Behavioral Interview

The hypothetical is just too "iffy" for some interviewers. This breed is more comfortable staying in the realm of the known, so they will dig deep into your past experience hoping to learn more about how you have already behaved in a variety of on-the-job situations. Then they'll attempt to use this information to extrapolate your future reactions on this job.

How did you handle yourself in some really tight spots? What kinds of on-the-job disasters have you survived? Did you do the right thing? What were the repercussions of your decisions?

Be careful of what you say. Every situation you faced was unique in its own way, so be sure to let the interviewer in on specific limitations you had to deal with. Did you lack adequate staff? Support from management? If you made the mistake of plunging in too quickly, say so and admit that you've learned to think things through. Explain what you'd do differently the next time around.

That said, my advice would be to steer away from the specifics of a particular situation and emphasize the personal strengths and expertise you'd feel comfortable bringing to any challenge you're likely to face.

4. The Team Interview

Today's organizational hierarchies are becoming flatter. That means that people at every level of a company are more likely to become involved in a variety of projects and tasks—including interviewing you for the job you're after.

How does this happen? That depends on the company. The team interview can range from a pleasant conversation to a torturous interrogation. Typically you will meet a group, or "team," of interviewers around a table in a conference room. They may be members of your prospective department or a cross-section of employees from throughout the company who you can expect to work with at some time or other in your new position.

The hiring manager or someone from human resources may chair an orderly session of question-and-answer—or turn the group loose to shoot questions at you like a firing squad. When it's all over, you'll have to survive the assessment of every member of the group.

Some hiring managers consult with the group after the interviewer for a "reading" on your performance. Others determine their decision using group consensus. The good news is that you don't have to worry that the subjective opinion of just one person will determine your shot at the job. Say one member of the group thinks you "lacked confidence" or came across as "arrogant." Others in the group may disagree. The interviewer who leveled the criticism will have to defend his or her opinion to the satisfaction of the group—or be shot down.

A group of people is also more likely (but not guaranteed) to ask you a broader range of questions that may uncover and underline your skills and expertise. Just take your time—and treat every member of the team with the same respect and deference you would the hiring manager.

Level Two: The Hiring Interview

You've made it this far. But don't relax yet. Your first interview with the person who will manage your prospective position is not likely to be a walk in the park. You may be stepping out of range of the experience and interviewing talent of the human resources professional—into unknown territory.

And you could wander there for a while.

Why? Experienced interviewers are trained to stay in charge of the interview, not let it meander down some dead-end, nonproductive track. There is a predictability to the way they conduct interviews, even when they wield different techniques.

A Little Knowledge is a Dangerous Thing

On the other hand, the hiring manager is sure to lack some or all of the screening interviewer's knowledge, experience and skill—making him or her an unpredictable animal.

The vast majority of corporate managers don't know what it takes to hire the right candidate. Few of them have had formal training in conducting interviews of any kind. To make things worse, most managers feel slightly less comfortable conducting the interview than the nervous candidate sitting across their desks from them!

For example, a manager might decide you are not the right person for the job, without ever realizing that the questions he or she asked were so ambiguous, or so off the mark, that even the perfect candidate could not have returned the "right" answer. No one monitors the performance of the interviewer. And the candidate cannot be a mind-reader. So more often than is necessary, otherwise perfectly qualified candidates are apt to walk out the door for good simply because the manager failed at the interview!

Foiling the Inept Interviewer

But that doesn't have to happen to you. You can—and should—be prepare to put your best foot forward, no matter what the manager who is interviewing for the job does or says. That begins with having the answers to 101 questions at the ready. But it doesn't stop there. Because the interviewer may not ask any of these questions.

What do you do then? In the chapters that follow, you'll see how you can give even the most dense of managers the feeling that you are the best person for the job.

Simply put, you're a step ahead of the game if you realize at the outset that managers who are interviewing to hire are after more than just facts about your skills and background. They are waiting for something more elusive to hit them, something they themselves may not be able to articulate. They want to feel that somehow you "fit" the organization or department.

Talk about a tough hurdle! But knowing what you're up against is half the battle. Rather than sit back passively and hope for the best, you can help the unskilled interviewer focus on how your unique skills can directly benefit—"fit"—the department or organization using a number of specific examples.

One word of caution. Don't come on so strong that you seem to be waging a campaign. You'll come off as overzealous and self-serving. You lose. Just keep quietly and confidently underlining the facts (your expertise) and enthusiastically showing (discovering together) how well these "puzzle pieces" seem to fit the job at hand.

That Certain Something

One afternoon, Alexander, my boss and the publishing director for the magazine I was running, asked me to stop by his office to meet a promising young candidate a friend had referred. "I know you don't have any positions open right now, Ron," he told me. "But could you take the time just to say hello?"

I was up to my ears with work, but I took a few moments to find out a little bit about Lynn. I asked her a few preliminary questions: Where she was working? What were her strengths? What she was looking for? I had planned to be out of there in five minutes.

But, somehow, we were still talking a half-hour later. By that time, I knew she was a terrific writer and editor. And I understood why she was thinking about making a move.

I still couldn't offer her a job. But she had impressed me so much in that informal meeting that when the managing editor spot opened up on my magazine a few months later, I didn't think twice. I called Lynn. After a more thorough and formal interview, she got the job.

What made Lynn such a winner? She displayed just those traits that I keep stressing, the traits employers are always looking for, no matter what the job description: confidence, enthusiasm, experience and dependability.

How to "Ace" Any Interview

- **Think of it as an adventure.** As opposed to a tribunal, that is. Try to enjoy it. Let the interviewer take on the status of a sports star, famous author or movie celebrity you've always admired in your mind. (Try to overlook the middle-aged paunch or glaring bald spot.) You'll still be nervous, but you'll be able to focus more on the job and the company. Believe me, that will do wonders to cultivate the interviewer's interest in you.

   I'm reminded of a friend of mine who was considering attending law school. Even though he hadn't yet made up his mind, he took the LSAT entrance examination—and scored pretty badly. Undaunted, he immediately signed up to take the exam again. But, by the time the next test date rolled around, another career option had his attention.

   Even so, he went ahead and took the LSAT again—for the experience (and, besides, he'd already paid the fee). This time he doubled his score! He wasn't any more prepared, but his attitude was different. Because he felt very little pressure to ace the test, he relaxed—and performed at his peak.

- **Keep smiling.** No matter what. Don't wear a pasted-on grin that will wear down to a grimace. Just maintain a pleasant, relaxed smile that is, hopefully, a byproduct of your involvement in an interesting conversation. Put yourself in the interviewer's place. Who wouldn't want to work with such an agreeable person?

- **Be enthusiastic.** About the position, your accomplishments and what you know about the company.

- **Be honest.** Don't gush about anything you're not genuinely enthusiastic about or you'll come across as a phony.

- **Make lots of eye contact.** Have you ever known someone who wouldn't look you in the eye? After a while, you probably started to wonder what that person had to hide. You don't want your interviewer wondering anything of the sort. So meet his or her eyes while you're shaking hands and then frequently throughout the interview. Don't stare so that you appear glassy-eyed. Unrelenting eye contact is just as bad as none at all.

- **Remain positive.** In other words, steer away from negative words as much as possible. As we'll see when we discuss questions about your previous jobs, you must learn to put a positive spin on everything, especially loaded issues, such as your reason for leaving a job, troubled relations with your superiors, and so on.

Here's a good exercise. Tape-record your answers to some of the questions in this book—and then write them down. How many negatives do you find "hidden" in your speech? Scratch them out and replace them with positive words and phrases. Then read and memorize each new answer.

- **Don't let an unskilled interviewer trip you up.** Make sure the confidence and preparation you've worked so hard for comes shining through—especially when a manager throws you a curve. Your preparation should give you the power to take control of the interview if need be.

Ready to get started? In the next chapter, we'll tackle the "killer" question.

Chapter 3

The Killer Question

1. So, tell me a little about yourself.

This is really more of a request than a question. But these few words can put you on the spot in a way no question can. And if you're unprepared for such an open-ended prelude to the series of standard questions about your skills, background and aspirations you've been expecting, it can stop you dead.

I'm not sure why this killer is a favorite of so many interviewers. But if you've escaped it thus far, count yourself lucky. You still have time to prepare! Chances are better than average that you will face it sometime soon.

Is the interviewer looking for specific clues? (Key words? Body language?) Or, as I have secretly suspected of many an unseasoned interviewer, is he or she simply looking for an easy to way to get the ball rolling?

At this point, it doesn't matter much to you. The spotlight is suddenly glaring in your eyes. Your pulse is racing, your throat parched. But if you're prepared, you know this can be your golden opportunity to *keep* the ball rolling by showing four of the traits the interviewer is scouting for: intelligence, enthusiasm, confidence and dependability.

Prepare to be Prepared

OK, it's time to dig out the personal inventory you completed in Chapter 1. (I told you it would be an important prerequisite for making good use of this book!) Study the items you've listed under these headings:

- My strongest skills.
- My greatest areas of knowledge.
- My greatest personality strengths.
- The things I do best.
- My key accomplishments.

Speech! Speech!

These topics will be the main ingredients of your opening statement. Be sure to make it short—about 250 to 350 words—and sweet—chock-full of specifics. It should take you no more than a minute or two to cover the following information:

1. Brief introduction.
2. Your key accomplishments.
3. The key strengths demonstrated by these accomplishments.

4. The importance of these strengths and accomplishments to your prospective employer.

5. Where and how you see yourself developing in the position for which you're applying (tempered with the right amount of modesty).

Barb's Bright Beginning

Let's dissect a couple of examples. Here is what Barb, a recent college graduate applying for an entry-level sales position, said:

*"I've always been able to **get along with different types of people**. I think it's because I'm a **good talker** and an even better **listener**.* (Modestly introduces herself, while immediately laying claim to the most important skills a good salesperson should have.)

*"When I began thinking seriously about which careers I'd be best-suited for during my senior year of high school, sales came to mind almost immediately. In high school and during my summers home from college, I worked **various part-time jobs at retail outlets*** (Demonstrates industriousness and at least some related experience.) *Unlike most of my friends, I actually **liked dealing with the public.*** (Conveys enthusiasm for selling.)

*"However, I also realized that retail had its limitations, so I went on to read about other types of sales positions. I was particularly **fascinated by what is usually described as consultative selling**. I like the idea of going to a client that you've really done your homework on and*

55

showing him how your products can help him solve one of his nagging problems and then following through on that. (Shows interest and enthusiasm for the scope of the job.)

"After I wrote a term paper on consultative selling in my senior year of college, I started looking for companies at which I could learn and refine the skills shared by people who are working as account executives rather than run-of-the-mill salespeople. (Shows initiative in researching both the area of consultative selling to write a term paper and then researching prospective companies.)

"That led me to your company, Mr. Shannon. I find the prospect of working with companies to increase the energy efficiency of their installations exciting. I've also learned some things about your sales training programs. They sound like they're on the cutting edge. (Gives evidence that she is an enthusiastic self-starter.)

"I guess the only thing I find a little daunting about the prospect of working at Co-generation, Inc., is selling that highly technical equipment without a degree in engineering. By the way, what sort of support does your technical staff lend to the sales effort? (Demonstrates that she is willing to learn what she doesn't know and closes by deferring to the interviewer's authority. By asking a question the interviewer must answer, Barb has also given herself a little breather. Now the conversational ball sits squarely in the interviewer's court.)

Not a bad little "speech" of a mere 281 words, is it?

Ken's Counter Punch

Now, let's look at one more example, before I leave you with some pointers on how you can write an effective opening tailored to your own personal inventory.

With nearly a decade of experience in his field, Ken is applying for his dream job as a district general manager for a firm that provides maintenance services to commercial and residential properties.

But going into the interview, he knows he has a couple of strikes against him. First of all, he's already held four jobs, so he's moved around a bit. And he doesn't yet have the management experience required by the job—virtually the equivalent of running a business with revenues of $7 million a year.

But because he has anticipated what might otherwise have been a devastating first job—"Tell me something that will help me get a better feel for you than I get here on the resume."—Ken is prepared with this winning counter punch:

"I'm a hard worker who loves this business. I've been an asset to the employers I've had, and my experience would make me an even greater asset to you.

"I think these are the most exciting times that I've ever seen in this business. Sure, there's so much more competition now, and it's harder than ever to get really good help. But all the indications are that more and more companies will out-source their maintenance needs and that more two-income households will require the services that we provide.

"How do we get a bigger share of this business? How do we recruit and train the best

personnel? Because they are, after all, the secret of our success. Those are the key challenges managers face in this industry.

"I can help your company meet those challenges. While resumes don't tell the whole story, mine demonstrates that:

"I'm a hard worker. I've had promotions at every company I've worked for.

"I would bring a good perspective to the position because I've been a doer, as well as a supervisor. The people who have worked for me have always respected my judgment, because they know I have a very good understanding of what they do.

"And I have a terrific business sense. I'm great at controlling expenses. I deploy staff efficiently. I'm fair. And I have a knack for getting along with customers.

"I've always admired your company. I must admit I have adopted some of CleanShine's methods and applied them in the companies I've worked for.

"I see now that you're branching into lawn care. I worked for a landscaping business during my high school summers. How is that business going?"

Way to go, Ken! In a mere 279 words, this successful candidate managed to:

1. **Focus the interviewer only on the positive aspects of his resume.** Sure, he has changed jobs. But, after this answer, the interviewer is likely to think, "Gee, look at all he's managed to accomplish everywhere he's gone."

2. **Get the interview started in the direction he wants it to go.** He demonstrated experience, leadership capabilities and a good understanding of the market.

3. **Introduce just the right amount of humility.** (While taking every opportunity to turn the spotlight on his many accomplishments and professional strengths.)

   As a result, Ken portrayed himself as a roll-up-the-sleeves type of manager who will be equally at ease with blue-collar workers as with the "suits" back at headquarters.

4. **Turn things back over to the interviewer with a very informed question.**

Keep Things Conversational

Although both Ken and Barb rehearsed their speeches, neither memorized them word for word. It's important to remember that the interviewer is not asking you to present a perfect essay, just to talk—person to person. Ken sprinkled in a little industry jargon here and there, which was entirely appropriate.

Just make sure you clearly and concisely communicate all five points I outlined previously.

Hey, Who's Running This Interview?

One of the most important things to note in Ken's reply is that he approached the interview knowing what he wanted to accomplish.

So many candidates spend hours selecting the right suit—only to sleepwalk through the interview. If you let the interviewer lead you in circles, you run the risk of ending up in a dead end.

Instead, Ken immediately assumed control, leading the interviewer, point by point, to the conclusion he hoped to reach.

It is essential for you to develop your own interview strategy, so your strengths can bob up to the surface and your weaknesses sink to the bottom. (Or, if they do surface, to give yourself the chance to make them seem relatively minor and unimportant.)

Getting Ready for the Killer Question

- **Complete your personal inventory.** If you bypassed the work in Chapter 1, go back and do it now, before we move on.

- **Distill your personal inventory into a compelling opening.** Use specifics to make this a short-and-sweet verbal picture of you, in which you frame yourself as an enthusiastic and competent professional—the ideal candidate for the job.

- **Don't memorize it, word-for-word.** You want to sound fresh—not like you're reading from a set of internal cue cards. So know the content. Record yourself speaking it until it sounds sincere, but spontaneous.

- **Include strong, positive phrases and words.** You want to convey enthusiasm and confidence as well as knowledge and experience. What you don't know, you're eager to learn.

- **Use it to set the course of the interview.** Anticipate that the "killer" will surface early in the interview, so be prepared to use it as an opportunity to steer the interview in the direction you want to take. Fine-tune your response—to give a positive shine to any potential negatives, such as apparent job-hopping and lack of related experience.

- **End with the ball in the interviewer's court.** By ending with a question, you get a much-deserved breather while, once again, demonstrating your involvement and enthusiasm.

Now that you're ready to survive the killer question, let's go on to what follows. More questions.

Chapter 4

What Have You Done With Your Life?

It shouldn't come as any surprise that most interview questions focus on your previous work experience. Many employers think that your past is "prologue" to your future performance. After all, if you do have some deep, dark character flaw, it's sure to have shown up before now.

So, be prepared to be thoroughly grilled. And to stay positive through it all. Let's look at some of the questions you're most likely to field.

---

2. Why are you thinking about leaving your current job?

Watch out for this one. It can be fatal.

Obviously, no one wants to leave a job they are completely content with. (Although some people routinely interview to stay in practice or stay in touch with what is currently on offer.)

But the last thing you want to do is appear negative or, worse, speak badly about your current employer. (Your interviewer will assume, fair or not, that, if hired, you'd talk the same way about your new employer as well.)

So handle your discontent (if that's what led you here) very gingerly. The less contented you are, the more careful you should be in talking about it. It will do you absolutely no good to confess to the interviewer that you lie awake nights fantasizing about putting a contract out on your current boss.

Instead, do some of what management consultants call "visioning." Imagine the ideal next step in your career. Then act as though you are interviewing for that position.

Here's what I mean. Say you're interested in assuming more financial management responsibilities. You might tell the interviewer:

> *"There is a great deal I enjoy about my current job. But my potential for growth in this area is limited at Closely Held, Inc., because of the size of the company and the fact that expansion is not a part of its current strategic plan."*

Bingo. Unless you have been fired or laid off, you should make it clear that you are sitting in front of the interviewer only because you seek more responsibility, a bigger challenge, better opportunities for growth—even more money—*not* because you are desperate to put some distance between yourself and your current job situation.

Out of Work, Not Out of Luck

> ## 3. Are you still employed at the last firm listed on your resume?

You probably know the adage that it's always easier to find a job when you already have one. It's still true.

But the fact is that massive layoffs seem to be the order if the day. So there is no shame in this status. And if you were fired? Come clean. But be quick to turn this potential negative into a positive.

Turning a Lemon Into Lemonade

Let's consider the case of Nick. A hotel sales manager, he was unfortunate enough to work for a petty tyrant who made a practice of taking Nick and his co-workers to task often, publicly and mercilessly.

One day, Nick finally had it. He blew up at his boss—and was fired on the spot. A few days later, he was asked about his employment status in an interview for another hotel sales job. He answered bluntly, "I was fired."

When the stunned interviewer asked to hear more, Nick explained:

> *"My boss and I just didn't get along, and I have to admit I didn't handle the situation very well."* He went on to cast the negative in a positive light. *"We have such vast differences in style. I'm someone with a lot of initiative who likes to be trusted to do a good job. Joe was highly structured, a very control-oriented manager who*

wanted the details on every sales call in triplicate."

"I certainly understand the importance of call reports and log sheets and other sales management controls. I guess I interpreted some of Joe's quick demands for these things as a lack of trust, and I shouldn't have. I learned my lesson."

Even the most fair-minded of interviewers tends to look on a firing or layoff as a sign of weakness. I even heard one experienced executive recruiter say, "Oh, if she was laid off, there must be something wrong with her. Companies don't ever let really good employees go!" Would that it were true!

So, if you have a blemish on your record, talk less about why you were terminated and more about what you've learned from the experience. And never dwell on the negative, such as what a rotten boss you had.

If you were laid off, or, as the British quaintly say, "made redundant," don't apologize. Say something like, "Yes, I was one of 16 people laid off when sales took a slide." (This is an easy way out—presuming you were not a member of the sales department!)

Do You Hop or Flop?

Some people have always had a job—in fact a lot of them. Yet companies are especially cautious about hiring people who have changed jobs repeatedly. Curiously enough, however, many are equally cautious of hiring people who have never moved. If either of these situations describes your particular job history, here's how to handle it.

---

4. After being with the same organization for so long, don't you think you might have a tough time getting accustomed to another?

Of course not! During your tenure with your current company, you've probably worked for more than one boss. You may even have supervised many different types of people in various departments. Certainly you've teamed up with a variety of co-workers. And from inside this one organization, you've had a chance to observe a wide variety of other organizations—competitors, vendors, customers and so on.

You're flexible—and loyal. You should remind the interviewer that this can prove a valuable combination.

---

5. You've changed jobs quite frequently. How do we know you'll stick around if we hire you?

---

6. You've been with your current employer for only a short amount of time. Is this an indication that you'll be moving around a lot throughout your career?

These questions are tougher. The hiring process is expensive for companies and time-consuming for managers. Job-hoppers only serve to make it a more frequent process.

So in framing your reply, convince the interviewer you have staying power by painting the position on offer as your career's "Promised Land." Here's how:

1. Confess that you had some difficulty defining your career goals at first, but now you are quite sure of your direction.

   -or-

2. Convince the interviewer that you left previous positions only after you realized that moving on was the only way to increase your responsibilities and broaden your experience.

Be sure to emphasize the fact that you would like nothing better than to stay and grow with a company.

Sherri's Situation

Sherri had four jobs in the first six years after college graduation. Her clever reply to an interviewer's skepticism about her staying power combines both techniques:

"All through college, I was convinced that I wanted to be a programmer. But after a few months in my first job, I found that I was unhappy. Naturally, I blamed the company and the job. So, when an opportunity opened up at Lakeside Bank, I grabbed it. But not long after the initial euphoria wore off, I was unhappy again.

"By this time I'd noticed that I really did enjoy the part of my job that dealt with applications. So when I heard about the job in end-user computing

at SafeInvest, I went for it. I learned a lot there, until I hit a 'glass ceiling.' It was a small firm, so there was no place for me to grow.

"I was recruited for the applications position at Deep Pockets Bank, and got it because of some of the innovations I'd developed at SI. The work has been terrific. But, once again, I find that I'm a one-person department.

"This position offers the opportunity to manage a department and interact with programmers and applications specialists on the cutting edge of technology. Throughout my career, the one thing that has remained constant is my love of learning. This job would give me the chance to learn so much."

Are You Management Material?

Fortunately (or unfortunately, depending on your point of view), moving up in most companies (and in most careers) means managing people.

If you are interviewing for a supervisory position or for a job that typically leads to a management track, the interviewer will try to probe your potential in this area.

---

7. Have you managed people in any of the positions you've held?

It's best to answer yes. Candidates with experience managing other people are considered more mature, whether or not their subordinates considered them good leaders. What's important is that they earned the confidence of their employers.

If this is you, be sure to give the interviewer specific details on how many people you supervised and in what capacities these people worked.

And if you haven't actually had people reporting to you? Talk about your experiences building consensus as part of self-managing teams. If these experiences have convinced you that you have the right stuff to be a good manager, by all means say so.

---

8. Have you been in charge of budgeting, approving expenses and monitoring departmental progress against financial goals? Are you very qualified in this area?

Again, financial responsibility signals an employer's faith in you. If you haven't had many—or any—fiscal duties, admit it. But as always, nothing is stopping you from being creative in the way you frame your reply. Here's an example:

> *"Well, I've never actually run a department, but I've had to set and meet budgetary goals for several projects I've worked on. In fact, I did this so often that I took a class to learn how to set up and use Lotus 1-2-3 spreadsheets."*

If you've had broader responsibilities, talk about your approval authority. What is the largest expenditure you could sign off on? Let the interviewer know, in round numbers, the income and expenses of the departments you've supervised.

9. How long have you been looking for a job?

Unless you've been fired or laid off, your answer should always be that you've just started looking. If you think the interviewer has some way of finding out that you've been looking for a while (perhaps you've come to him through a recruiter who knows your history), be prepared to explain why you haven't received or accepted any offers.

10. Why haven't you received any offers so far?

You're just as choosy about finding the right job as the interviewer is about hiring the right candidate. Don't whine or show that the search is upsetting you. If you've already fielded an offer or two, you might say:

"I have had an offer. But the situation was not right for me. I'm especially glad that I didn't accept, since I now have a shot at landing this position."

It's important to tell the truth, however, because the interviewer's next logical question may be the following.

11. Who made you the offer? For what type of position?

If you've already lied, you're in hot water now!

Many interviewers know a great deal about their competitors and which positions they're trying to fill. If you did the smart thing and told the truth, do give the interviewer the name of the company.

It's very important to stress that the position you turned down was very similar to the one you're applying for now. After all, if the job you're currently interviewing for is perfect for you—as you've undoubtedly told the interviewer three or four times already—why would you be at all interested in something very different at the other company?

Tips for Answering Questions About Work

- **Be positive about your reason for leaving your current job**. Or any previous jobs, for that matter. The key word to remember is "more." You want *more* responsibility, *more* challenges, *more* opportunity and finally, (but don't play this up) *more* money.

- **If you've been fired, stress what you learned from the experience.** Be as positive as you can.

- **Quantify the confidence other employers have placed in you.** Do this by stressing specific facts, figures and measurable accomplishments. Mention the number of employees you've supervised, the amount of money you controlled, the earnings that your department achieved under your management.

- **Never speak badly of past supervisors or employers.**

- **Make the job you're interviewing for your chief objective.** Frame your answers so that you let the interviewer know that you see this job as a means to achieving your ultimate career objectives. Be careful not to make it sound like either a stepping stone or a safe haven.

OK, you've demonstrated your experience. But how will you use what you know in the job you're applying for? What personal strengths do you bring to the table that set you apart from the crowd of applicants this interviewer may yet see?

Chapter 5

Work—and the *Real* You

Now that the quantitative data about your past experience managing people, handling money and generally taking them by storm is out of the way, it's time to get down to the nitty-gritty. How did you do it? What makes you different from someone else with the same responsibilities and record?

In a sense, you'll be asked to assess your own career performance. So think carefully about how you answer each of the following questions. Screening interviewers and hiring managers will use information you volunteer about how you handled past triumphs—and tribulations—to draw conclusions about how you may handle tough situations you'll encounter in the job at hand.

Your Strengths and Weaknesses

> **12. What are your strengths as an employee?**

13. Why should I consider you a strong applicant for this position?

To prepare for these questions, pull out those Data Input Sheets you labored over in Chapter 1 and write down the description of the position you're interviewing for. This will help you clarify each specific job requirement in your mind. Now, match your strengths and accomplishments directly to the requirements of the job.

Say that you have a singular skill for meeting even the most unreasonable deadlines. You are tenacious. Nothing can stop you. This job may require a different sort of tenacity. You may have to coddle and cajole a wide variety of managers in several offices across the country to get input for the documents you produce—and then follow through by getting each and every one to sign off on the finished product.

The interviewer may even admit that, frankly, deadlines often "slip" in this company. The important thing is that documents are "universally" approved. You need the perseverance to keep on plugging until that happens. If you go on at length about each "under-the-wire" experience, you just talk yourself right out of a job.

Are there any gaps? Probably a few—especially if you're reaching for the challenge at the next level of your career. So, now it's time to dig in and deal with the hard questions you know, by now, will be right on the tail of the ones above.

14. What are your biggest weaknesses as an employee?

15. What do you plan to do to correct those weaknesses?

16. What are the biggest failures you've had during your career?

17. What have you done to make sure they won't occur again?

18. What are the skills you most need to develop to advance your career?

And also,

19. What do your supervisors tend to criticize most about your performance?

20. How did you do on your last performance appraisal? What were the key strengths and weaknesses mentioned by your supervisor?

Before you start to spill your guts, remember that the interviewer is not a priest. This is not a confessional! In this situation, it would be foolhardy to produce a detailed log of your shortcomings and missteps for the interviewer. But it would be equally silly to pretend you're perfect and have never experienced failure in the course of your career, education or life.

So, compromise. The best approach is to admit to one weakness or failure—make it a good one!—and then talk about the steps you are taking (or have taken) to make sure that you'll never fail in that way again.

What makes a "good" weakness? Good question! Choose any deficiency that might be considered a plus in a slightly different light. For example:

- You have a tendency to take on too much yourself. You're trying to solve this problem by delegating more.
- You're impatient with delays. So you're trying to better understand every step of the process a product must go through so you can anticipate hold-ups in the future.
- You've realized you're a workaholic. But you're doing your best to remedy your "condition" by reading books on time management.

Try to think of a failure that took place relatively early in your career and/or one that would seem completely unrelated to the work you would be performing for your new employer.

Don't ever admit to any personal quality that might hamper job performance, such as procrastination, laziness or lack of concentration.

Dealing with the Boss

> **21. Tell me about the best/worst boss you've ever had.**

Talk about loaded questions! You could try for an on-the-spot description of the hiring manager sitting across the desk from you—and hope it's also on the money.

But as a rule of thumb, most companies want to hear that you most enjoyed working for someone who was interested in helping you learn and grow, involved in monitoring your progress and generous about giving credit when it was due. I hope you've had the chance to work for someone like that!

Now, what do you say about your *worst* boss? Don't get carried away with venomous accusations. They may serve only to introduce doubt about your own competence or ability to get along with other people.

For example, if you level the charge of "favoritism," the interviewer might wonder why your boss liked other employees more than you. If you complain about a boss who was always looking over your shoulder, the interviewer might wonder whether it was because you couldn't be trusted to complete a task accurately or on time.

Again, make sure to whitewash any negatives. Spend most of your time accentuating your positive experiences, accomplishments and qualities. If you say that your boss was "stingy with his knowledge," you are implying your desire to learn. In the same vein, saying that a supervisor was "uninvolved" could indicate your desire to work within a cohesive team. Just prepare—and practice—your response ahead of time.

---

22. Looking back on the experience now, do you think there was anything you could have done to improve your relationship with that one bad boss?

Of course you do. The work experience you've had since has shown you how to better accept criticism. Now that you have a better understanding of the pressures your supervisors are under, you can more successfully anticipate their needs. Use this opportunity to demonstrate your experience, perceptiveness and maturity.

How Well Do You Fit In?

In the world of business, "style" has little to do with how well you dress. (Although at some companies, and in some positions, the "right" wardrobe may be a defining element of the culture.) Typically, your business style is a measure—and often a subjective measure, at that—of how you conduct yourself on the job.

How well do you get along with superiors? Subordinates? Peers? What's your management philosophy? Do you like to work alone or be part of a team? Although they may try to be as objective as possible, many interviewers will base at least some of their hiring decision on their feelings about your attitude—and how well it is likely to fit within the organization. They may ask the following questions to find out whether you and the company are likely to be a good match in terms of work style:

---

23. Are you an organized person?

Even if you firmly believe that a neat desk is the sign of a sick mind, talk in detail about the organizational skills that you have developed—time management, project management, needs assessment, delegation—and the how those skills have made you more effective.

24. Do you manage your time well?

I hope you can truthfully say yes—that you are a self-starter and almost never procrastinate. Good employees are able to set goals, prioritize their tasks and devote adequate, and appropriate, amounts of time to each one.

However, in answering a rather conceptual question like this one (and what could be more conceptual than time?), try to sprinkle in specifics. Here are a few examples:

> *"I rarely miss a deadline. When circumstances beyond my control interfere, I make up the time lost as quickly as possible."*

> *"I establish a 'To Do' list first thing in the morning. Then I add to it—and re-prioritize tasks, if necessary—as the day goes on.*

> *"I really like interacting with the people I work with. But when I need to focus on detailed tasks, I make sure to set aside time that will be free of interruptions of any kind, so I can concentrate and work more effectively."*

25. How do you go about making important decisions?

By now, you have some sense of the culture in the company you're interested in working for. So shade your answer to match it.

For example, if you want to work for a financial services company, you probably don't want to portray yourself as a manager who makes decisions based on "gut feel," over hard data. Similarly, if you're auditioning to be an air traffic controller, it's best not to admit that you like to "sleep" on things before making up your mind.

Think in terms of the interviewer's main concerns. Will you need to be analytical? Creative? Willing to call on the expertise of others?

If you are bucking for a management position, you'll also want to take this opportunity to convince the interviewer that your relationship skills have made you management material—or set you on the way to achieving that goal.

You might say something like this: "When I'm faced with an important decision, I ask the advice of others. I try to consider everything. But, ultimately, I'm the one who decides. I guess that's why they say, 'It's lonely at the top.' The higher you go in management, the more responsibility you have and the more decisions you have to make by yourself."

26. Do you work well under pressure?

Naturally, everyone will say yes to this question. However, it will be best to provide examples that support your claims about your cool head under fire. Be sure to choose anecdotes that don't imply that the pressure you've faced has resulted from your own procrastination or failure to anticipate problems.

27. Do you anticipate problems well or merely react to them?

All managers panic from time to time. The best learn to protect themselves by looking for problems that might lie around the bend. For example, one sales manager I know had his staff provide reports on all positive—and negative—budget variances on a weekly basis. By sharing this valuable information not only to his boss, but also with the manufacturing, distribution and marketing arms of the company, he helped improve product turnover and boost flagging sales. This kind of story is terrific fodder for successful interviews.

---

28. Would you describe yourself as a risk-taker or someone who plays it safe?

In most cases, the ideal candidate will be a little of both. Interviewers who ask this question are probing for innovation and creativity. Are you a leader or a sheep? But they also want to find out whether you might turn into a "loose cannon" who will ignore company policies and be all too ready to head off into uncharted waters.

If You Could Do It Over...

Interviewers use hypothetical questions to get candidates to think on their feet. They expect you to "know your lines" when it comes to the facts about your career and education. But how will you react when you have to drop your guard and ad lib?

---

29. If you could start your career all over again, what would you do differently?

---

30. What is the biggest mistake you've ever made in choosing a job? Why?

Unless you're shooting for a complete change of career, you must convince the interviewer that you wouldn't change a thing. You love your career and, given the chance, you'd do it all over.

Regrets? We've all had a few. In this case, however, watch which ones you mention and make sure you position them in a way that shows what you've learned. Did you leave your first job because you were too impatient for a promotion, only to realize you hadn't learned all you could have? Did you miss the opportunity to specialize in some area or develop a particular expertise that you should have?

It certainly isn't advisable to admit, "I wish I had never gotten into magazine publishing in the first place. But now I guess I'm stuck. And to think, I could have been editing garden books for FernMoor Press..."

Better to reply: "My only regret is that I didn't go in this direction sooner. I started my career in editorial, and I enjoyed that. But once I got into marketing, I found I really loved it. Now, I can't wait to get to work every day."

Love 'em—or Tolerate 'em?

---

31. Do you prefer to work with others, or by yourself?

---

32. Are you good with people?

---

33. How do you get along with superiors?

---

34. How do you get along with co-workers?

---

35. How do you get along with people you've supervised?

Again, the position you're interviewing for will dictate how you should shape your answers. For example, if you're interviewing for a job as an on-the-road, far-corners sales rep, you won't want to say that you thrive on your relationships with co-workers and can't imagine working without a lot of interaction.

Even if you do like the interaction at work, don't try to paint your environment as a bed of roses without any thorns. You know the old saying: "You can choose your friends, but you can't choose your relatives." Often that goes for co-workers, too.

Every job situation forces us to get along with people we might not choose to socialize with. But we must get along with them, and, quite often, for long stretches of time and under difficult circumstances. Acknowledging this shows strength. Talk about how you've managed to get along with a wide variety of other people.

Once I was interviewing candidates for manager of a production department with 16 employees. Production departments in publishing companies are filled with some of the quirkiest people you'll ever come across, so I had to gauge the people skills of each applicant very carefully.

After I'd asked one candidate a couple of the questions about his management and communication skills, he gave me a steady look and said:

"Look, you know and I know it's not always easy to manage artists and proofreaders. I do my best to convince them of the importance of deadlines and let them know what it costs us when we miss them. I also point out how unfair it is to others in the department, and to the entire operation, when things are held up unnecessarily.

"I usually find some way to get along with all of the people in the department, some way to convince them that timeliness and accuracy are absolute musts. It's not always easy. But a lot of times it's fun. When we are rushed because of another department is late, I use this as an object lesson. The most important thing is to distribute the work fairly and let everyone know that you expect them to do their share."

Tips for Handling Questions About Work

- **Be honest.** But, again, play up your strengths and whitewash your weaknesses. If you have to talk about negative experiences, point out what you learned from them, and why you won't make the same mistakes again.

- **Introduce only the positive.** Don't give away information that could come back to haunt you.

- **Strike a balance between portraying yourself as a "company man or woman" and a "loose cannon."** Screening interviewers and hiring managers are often attracted to risk-takers. But they also put a lot of stock in playing by the rules.

- **Use specific work situations to illustrate your points.** If you sense the interview drifting into the realm of the subjective evaluation, plan to bring the interviewer back by using concrete examples from your past experience. Don't just say you're organized. Tell how you organized a complex project from beginning to end.

- **Choose your words carefully.** Make sure that you are indeed answering questions, and not suggesting other areas the interviewer hadn't thought to explore. For example, I suggest, "I'm looking for greater challenges," rather than, "The boss didn't give me enough to do."

Congratulations! You've successfully cleared another interview hurdle. Now you're on to the next. It's time to talk—in detail—about your current job.

Chapter 6

Why Are
You Here?

In most prizefights, the first couple of rounds are relatively boring. The contestants spend this time checking each other out—trying to get a sense for each other's feints and jabs—before the serious pummeling begins.

The same could be said of most interviews. After the first bell, the pleasantries begin. The second bell signals the "getting-to-know-you" round of questioning. Then, if the interviewer thinks it's worthwhile, he begins "pummeling" you—with questions meant to separate the "stiffs" from the prize candidates.

Put on Your Gloves

Up until now, the questions have been tough. But the "fight" ahead promises to get even tougher. You'll have to prepare to come out swinging.

---

36. What were your most memorable accomplishments in your last job? Of your career?

Focus on your most recent accomplishments—in your current position or the job you had just previous to this one. But make sure they are relevant to the position you're interviewing for.

For example, a friend of mine, who had been an editor for years, answered this question by talking at length about the times she'd been asked to write promotional copy for the marketing department. She was trying to change careers so she deliberately tried to shift the interviewer's attention from her editing experience to her accomplishments as a marketing copywriter.

It's also wise to think about why you were able to achieve these peaks in your career.

For example:

"I really stopped to listen to what my customers wanted, rather than just trying to sell them."

"I realized that I needed to know a lot more about Sub-chapter S corporations, so I enrolled in a tax seminar."

This type of response tells the interviewer you give a great deal of thought to how you will reach your goals rather than blindly plunging ahead in their general direction. By letting the interviewer know that you are in the practice of regularly assessing your shortcomings, you show that you are better able to find the means to overcome them.

Are You an Innovator?

Remember that most employers are looking for problem-solvers. A savvy interviewer may ask this question after you've described your reasons for leaving your current job, wondering why you didn't try to come up with a way to fix what was "broke."

---

37. Was there anything your company (or department) could have done to be more successful?

---

38. Did you inaugurate any new procedures (or systems or policies) in any of the positions you've held?

Of course. You had some very good solutions you'd be happy to share with the interviewer. Regrettably, however, some (or none?) could be implemented because of circumstances beyond your control.

This is the time to bring up those facts and figures we talked about earlier. Describe the changes or improvements you were responsible for making and identify how they helped the company, in terms of increased profits, costs savings or improved production.

Here's a perfectly acceptable answer:

> *"Sure, we could have expanded our product line, perhaps even doubled it, to take advantage of our superior distribution. But we just didn't have the capital and couldn't get the financing."*

> **39. What is the title of the person you report to, and what are his or her responsibilities?**

> **40. Describe the way your department is organized.**

Aha! Gotcha! If you've been exaggerating the responsibilities of your position, you're about to be found out. To prevent this embarrassing moment, don't portray your job as so big that there couldn't be anything left for your boss to do.

What Will Become of You?

Is desperation driving you away from your current job, so that you'll say or do anything to get this one? This doesn't paint an attractive picture of you for the interviewer. So, be sure you are the picture of composure and control, whatever your situation.

> **41. If you don't leave your current job, what do you think will happen to you in your career? How far do you expect to advance with your current company?**

Remember the adage: "There's no better time to look for a new job than when you're happy with your old job." Even if you'd rather hawk peanuts at the stadium than stay another month at ABC Widget, convince the interviewer that you're the type of employee who is capable of making the most of any situation—even an employment situation you've just said you want to leave.

You could say: "Naturally I'm interested in this job and have been thinking about leaving ABC. However, my supervisors think highly of me, and I expect that one day other situations will open up for me at the company. I'm one of ABC's top salespeople. I have seen other people performing at similar levels advance to management positions. That's what I'm looking for right now."

Whatever your feeling about your current job, it's always best to conduct your part of the interview as if you are in the driver's seat, just cruising along happily until you see that changing lanes would improve your career. You don't want to rush into anything.

Begin your answers with the phrase, "Well, assuming I'm not the successful candidate for this position..." Without too much ego, let the interviewer know that you're taking your time. You're interested in choosing a job that's right for you.

If You're so Happy, Why are You Here?

While it's a good idea to convince your prospective employer that the world is your oyster—and you're simply waiting to find the perfect pearl of a job—you might get hit with questions like these:

---

42. If you're so happy at your current firm, why are you looking for another job? Will they be surprised that you're leaving?

You might think your current company will go out of business at any second. Or you may be leaving because you just broke off your engagement with the person in the office next door. Don't cry on the interviewer's shoulder.

Instead, reassure him or her that you not running away from anything. You've made the decision to move toward:

- More responsibility.
- More knowledge.
- The wonderful opportunity available at Good Times, Inc.

---

43. If you have these complaints about your present company, and they think so highly of you, why haven't you brought your concerns to their attention?

Some problem-solver you are! You can't even talk to your boss about changes that might make you happier!

If you do find yourself cornered, facing this dead end, the only way out is to be as positive as possible. Say something like, "Grin & Bear It is aware of my desire to move up. But the company is still small. There's really not much they can do about it. The management team is terrific. There's no need right now to add to it, and they are aware of some of the problems this creates in keeping good performers. It's something they talk about quite openly."

More Tips for Interview Success

- **Shape your responses to the position.** Learn as much as you can about the position you're interviewing for—before you get to the interview. When you talk about your own accomplishments, skills and experience, talk in terms of the requirements of the job—and the goals of the company.

- **Always think in terms of what—and why.** As you talk about your accomplishments—or failures—stress the positive lessons you've learned that you've already applied or plan to apply in your next position.

- **Don't exaggerate.** Your accomplishments and responsibilities should speak for themselves. If you felt you lacked opportunities to make a mark in the past, say so. If you bend the truth, there are too many ways a savvy interviewer can find you out, so don't learn the hard way.

- **Don't appear desperate.** Even if you've been terminated from your previous job! But don't come across as smug, either. Concentrate on expressing your genuine interest and enthusiasm for the opportunities offered by the job on offer—such as more responsibility, more knowledge and more money.

- **Avoid the negative.** You want the interviewer to associate as few negative words or feelings with you as possible.

- **Make the best of your current position.** Let the interviewer know you may still be able to find some of the things you're looking for in your current position. You want to convey the impression that you are a positive worker who tries to make the best of any situation.

- **Build a vocabulary of action words.** The following words are strong and positive. If you use them consistently in your resume, interviews and follow-up letters, they should leave a lasting impression in the interviewer's mind.

  Take a few moments to review these words each day, even after you're off the interview circuit. In very little time, they'll find their way into your speaking and writing.

Words that Pack a Professional Punch

Ability	Compared	Detected
Accelerated	Compiled	Determined
Accomplished	Completed	Developed
Accurate	Conceived	Directed
Achieved	Conceptualized	Discovered
Adjusted	Conducted	Disproved
Administered	Consolidated	Distributed
Advised	Constructed	Edited
Analyzed	Consulted	Effective
Approved	Controlled	Eliminated
Arranged	Coordinated	Energy
Assisted	Counseled	Enlarged
Built	Created	Enthusiasm
Calculated	Decreased	Established
Capable	Delivered	Evaluated
Charted	Designed	Examined

Excelled
Expanded
Focus
Formulated
Founded
Generated
Guided
Headed
Identified
Implemented
Improved
Increased
Initiated
Inspected
Installed
Instituted
Instructed
Interpreted
Introduced
Invented
Justified
Launched
Lead
Lectured
Led
Made
Maintained
Managed

Modified
Monitored
Motivated
Negotiated
Obtained
Operated
Ordered
Organized
Performed
Persuaded
Planned
Prepared
Presented
Prided
Processed
Produced
Proficiency
Programmed
Promoted
Proposed
Provided
Purchased
Recommended
Reduced
Referred
Reorganized
Replaced
Reported

Represented
Researched
Responsible
Restored
Reviewed
Revised
Scheduled
Selected
Served
Sold
Solved
Streamlined
Strengthened
Studied
Supervised
Supplied
Systematic
Taught
Tested
Thorough
Trained
Translated
Updated
Urgency
Utilized
Vital
Won
Wrote

So, now the bright light has been turned, full-force, on your current work situation. It got pretty hot at times. But you've survived again to enter the next round. At the next bell, you'll show off what you know about the job you're interviewing for—and your prospective company.

Chapter 7

OK, Off With Your Defenses

Now we come to a classic good news/bad news scenario.

First, the good news. If you've made it to this point, the interviewer probably likes you. Most screening interviewers and hiring managers weed out the candidates who don't stand a chance long before they get to the questions in this and the following chapters.

Now, for the bad news. The interviewer will continue grilling you—with renewed gusto—until the facade you've been bravely holding up finally starts to crumble.

So suck up your stamina. (If you're lucky, you'll have a few days to rest up—and worry—before your second interview.)

Here goes.

---

44. What interests you most about this position? This company?

---

101 Interview Questions

You know the drill from some of the previous chapters. You have your eye on more responsibility, more opportunities, the chance to supervise more people, the chance to develop a new set of skills and sharpen the ones you've already acquired.

However, this is also the ideal time to show what you know about this company, and how the position you're interviewing for can contribute to its success.

You'll have to do some homework to get the answers to these questions:

- What are the company's leading products? What products is it planning to introduce in the near future?
- What are the company's key markets? Are they growing? Changing?
- What is the company's share of its market?
- Which other companies serving those markets (competitors) pose a serious threat?
- What are the company's plans and prospects for growth and expansion?

Armed with this knowledge, you might reply: "I've heard so much about your titanium ball bearings that I've wanted to experiment with different applications for them." Rather than, "I'll have a better commute if I get this job." (Unbelievably, I've heard this response from more than one candidate I've interviewed!)

Doing some preliminary research also will give you a leg up should the interviewer ask:

---

45. What have you heard about our company that you _don't_ like?

This is tricky. So opt for a response that doesn't relate directly to the job you're after. Maybe you've heard that ABC Widget had a layoff 12 months ago and are wondering if the dust has settled yet. Or you've heard rumors of a merger.

Don't play dumb. Any new prospect would have reservations about the company's stability and plans for the future. If the interviewer opens the door for you to ask what might otherwise be uncomfortable questions, by all means take advantage of it.

---

46. This is a much larger (or smaller) company than you've ever worked at. How do you feel about that?

If the company is larger, you are undoubtedly looking forward to terrific growth opportunities and exposure to more areas of knowledge than you have access to now.

If the prospective company is smaller, you are looking forward to a far less bureaucratic organization, where decisions can be made much more quickly and where no department is so large that it is not extremely familiar with the workings of the entire company.

---

47. What aspect of the job I've described appeals to you the least?

Let me lead with a little humor. After conversing with his Irish friend one day, a man finally blurted out in consternation, "Why do the Irish always answer a question with a question?" Unruffled, the Irishman winked and replied, "Do we now?"

Your best tactic is to follow suit. Shoot the question right back at the interviewer!

For example, you might say, "You've described a position in which I'd be overseeing some extraordinary levels of output. What sort of quality-control procedures does this company have? Will I be able to consult with in-house specialists?"

Talking about Ideals

> **48. Based on what you know about our industry right now, how does your ideal job stack up against the description of the job you're applying for?**

The "ideal" job is always one in which you'll have a broad scope of responsibilities that will enable you to continue to learn about your industry and grow. So use your knowledge about the industry to formulate a reply that might sound a bit idealistic, without being unrealistic.

Here's an example:

"I know that many accounting firms are deriving more and more of their fee income from consulting services. I'd like a job that combines my cost accounting knowledge with client consultation and problem-solving. Ideally, I'd like to start as part of a team, then eventually head up a practice in a specific area, say cost accounting in manufacturing environments."

Now, based on what you know about the position, touch on one (and only one) minor shortcoming, and formulate a few careful questions about some aspects of the position you don't know about. Expanding on the above example, you might say:

"I know this position is in the auditing area and that you hire many of your entry-level people into that department. I must confess I would like this to be a stepping stone to working more in the manufacturing area and, several years down the line, in consulting. I'm sure I don't have the requisite knowledge or experience yet. Is this a position in which I can gain such experience, and is this a career track that's possible at this firm?"

Your Perspective on People

---
49. What types of people do you find it most difficult to get along with?

What a land mine this might be! Be careful. You might say, "Pushy, abrasive people," only to find out the interviewer is known for being "brusque."

One candidate I interviewed gave me what I thought was a good answer to this question:

"I was discussing this problem with my boss just the other day," she said. "He told me I'm too impatient with slow performers. He told me that the world is filled with 'C,' rather than 'A' or 'B' people, and I expect them all to be great performers. So, I guess I do have trouble with mediocre and poor workers."

---

50. Are there any people that have trouble getting along with you?

If you say no, the interviewer will assume you're being evasive. So, be ready with an answer. I suggest thinking of an anecdote—a short story that softens with humor the reasons someone disliked you.

A colleague of mine remembered back to his first job. Just out of college, he was the first new hire in his department within a state agency in six years. Eager to succeed, he hit the ground running. From day one, he worked twice as fast as his long-term peers, who, needless to say, resented him for it. So, his answer was ready-made.

Trial by Fire-ing

If you've ever been a manager, you probably hired and fired people. But even if you haven't yet been blessed with those responsibilities, here are some suggestions for responding to the following questions.

---

51. Have you ever hired anyone? Why did you choose him or her (or them)?

If you have hired one or more people during your career, your answer might go something like this:

"Yes, I have hired people. I have also decided whether some internal applicants were right for jobs in my department. The first time I hired

someone, I concentrated on checking off all the right qualifications. I just went down a checklist.

"Since then, though, I've learned that some candidates who became excellent workers didn't necessarily have every qualification on that checklist. They more than make up for what they lacked in the beginning with enthusiasm and a willingness to work with others."

What if you've never hired anyone? You might try this tack:

"Not really. But on several occasions I was asked to speak to prospective applicants and offer my opinion. Of course, in those cases, I was trying to determine whether that person would be a team player and if he or she would get along with the other people in the department."

---

52. Have you ever fired anyone? Why?

Even if you had good reason, you know that firing someone is never pleasant. Say so, and provide a "sanitized," (and brief!) version of the events to the interviewer.

Remember, you don't want to seem like a negative person, one who might disrupt an entire department. But don't overdo the sympathy either—going on and on about some poor, out-of-work subordinate.

Let's say you fired someone for not meeting productivity goals. You might be thinking, "And boy, I'm glad I got rid of that bum. He was nothing but a wimp and whiner who never did a good day's work in all the time he was in the job." Go ahead and think that. But when you open your mouth, say something like this:

> *"Yes, I fired someone who continually fell short of his productivity goals. His shortcomings were documented and discussed with him over a period of months. But, in that time he failed to show any real improvement. I had no choice. As a supervisor, I want everyone in my department to work out. Let's face it, though, not everyone is equally dedicated to his or her job."*

If you haven't actually fired anyone, here's one way to respond:

> *"I've never actually fired anyone myself, but it was the policy at my company that no hirings or firings should be unilateral. I was asked on two occasions to give my opinion about someone else's performance. It's never easy to be honest about a co-worker's shortcomings. But I felt I had to do what was best for the department and fair to everyone else in it."*

Your Definition of Success

---

53. What does the word "success" mean to you?

Answer this question from a personal as well as professional perspective. If your successes come only through your job, the interviewer might begin to see you as little more than an automaton. However, if you go on and on about the personal goals you have, you'll seem uncommitted to working for success on the job.

Strike a balance. You might talk about success in these terms:

> *"I have always enjoyed supervising a design team. In fact, I've discovered that I'm better at working with other designers than designing everything myself. Unlike a lot of the people in my field, I'm also able to relate to the requirements of the manufacturing department.*
>
> *"So, I guess I'd say success means working with others to come up with efficient designs that can be up on the assembly line quickly. Of course, the financial rewards of managing a department give me the means to travel during my vacations. That's the thing I love most in my personal life."*

---

54. What does the word "failure" mean to you?

It's better to use a specific example to demonstrate what you mean by "failure." Otherwise, you might get into a lengthy philosophical discussion more suited to a Bergman film than an interview.

Here's a good answer:

> *"Failure is not getting the job done when I have the means to do so. For example, once I was faced with a huge project. I should have realized at the outset that I didn't have the time. I must have been thinking there were 48 hours in a day! I also didn't have the knowledge I needed to do it*

correctly. Instead of asking some of the other people in my department for help, I blundered through. That won't ever happen to me again if I can help it!"

The Not-so-elusive Future

Here's one that makes everybody cringe. It's not that you don't have plans, but things can change substantially in the space of five years, altering even the loftiest goals. So keep it simple—be positive and vague.

> ## 55. What do you want to be doing five years from now? What are your most important long-term goals?

Of course, you want a position of responsibility in your field. But you don't want to appear overly ambitious. So, start humbly:

"Well, ultimately that will depend on my performance on the job and on the growth and opportunities offered by my employer."

Then, toot your own horn a little bit:

"I've already demonstrated leadership characteristics in all of the jobs I've held, so I feel confident that I will take on progressively greater management responsibilities in the future. That suits me fine. I enjoy building a team, developing its goals and then working to accomplish them. It's very rewarding."

---

56. Have you recently established any new objectives or goals?

This question provides you an opportunity to demonstrate how your goals and motivations have changed as you've matured and gained valuable work experience. If you've recently become a manager, talk about how that experience has affected your career outlook for the future. If you've realized that you must sharpen a particular skill to continue growing, mention that.

Dictator—or Pushover?

Interviewers want to be sure that, as a manager, you'll be neither.

---

57. How would you describe your management philosophy?

You want to demonstrate a desire and ability to delegate, teach and distribute work—and credit—fairly.

Don't use some of these wishy-washy answers I've actually heard during interviews:

> *"I try to get people to like me, and then they really work hard for me."*

> *"I guess you could say I'm a real people-person."*

Do give an answer that conveys authority and experience:

> *"More than anything else, I think that management is getting things done through other*

people. The manager's job is to provide the resources and environment in which people can work effectively. I try to do this by creating teams, judging people solely on the basis of their performance, distributing work fairly and empowering workers, to the extent possible, to make their own decisions. I've found that this breeds loyalty and inspires hard work."

Tips for Convincing the Interviewer You're a Good Catch

- **Do your homework**. Find out as much as you can about the company and how the position you're interviewing for contributes to its goals.
- **Demonstrate experience—and exude confidence.** Give the interviewer strong answers, using examples that are relevant to the position you're after.
- **Be humble**. Convey the impression that you have the ability to succeed, should opportunities present themselves.
- **Appear firm, but not dictatorial.** When you talk about your management philosophy, let the interviewer know that you are able to delegate, and still keep track of each person's progress.
- **Talk about growth.** Tell the interviewer how you've grown in each of the jobs you've held and how your career goals have changed as a result.
- **Admit to your failures.** But concentrate on what you learned from them, using examples to show how you've changed as a result of what you've learned.
- **Showcase your successes.** As a professional with a satisfying personal life.

Chapter 8

Let's Get Personal

Most people think that the candidate who talks only about work, work, work stands the best chance of getting the job. But there's a "you" that exists after 5 p.m.—and most interviewers want to get to know that person, too.

The guiding principle for answering personal questions is the same as it is for responding to queries about your professional experiences: Emphasize the positive. Let the interviewer in on the best and most interesting aspects of your personality.

The Double-edged Sword

Just be careful of saying too much. Your answers can reveal more information than the interviewer is entitled by law to ask for. For example, in the warm glow of an interview that seems to be going well, you might feel comfortable talking about your children—and the challenges of being a single parent.

The interviewer could not have asked about your family situation, in order to eliminate you from the running. Yet once this information is out, it's fair game. He or she is free to use it to make unfair judgments about your ability to handle various aspects of the job. If the job you're applying for involves occasional overnight travel, for example, he or she may decide your family situation would create unnecessary difficulties.

So, while these questions do give you an opportunity to demonstrate what a terrific person you are, they could also prompt you to—unwittingly—provide information that does you in as a prospective candidate for employment!

To Your Good Health

Employers have more than just a passing interest in your health. Most companies are looking for ways to keep the overall cost of health care insurance from skyrocketing. Most managers want to know that you won't be felled by every flu bug that makes the rounds—and on sick leave when they need you most.

---

58. Are you in good health? What do you do to stay in shape?

You must be honest in answering this one. Prospective employers can easily check your medical history by contacting your insurance carrier. In fact, many employers make job offers contingent on your passing a physical examination.

If you appear to be dedicated to maintaining your own good health, you'll ease many of their concerns. You don't have to be an exercise nut. Just play up any activities you do regularly that provide at least some health benefit, such as yard work, home repairs, even walking the dog.

> ### 59. Do you have any physical problems that may limit your ability to perform this job?

This is a perfectly legitimate question for the interviewer to ask. So be honest. Are you applying for a job that requires a lot of data entry despite the fact that you've been waging an ongoing battle with carpal tunnel syndrome for some time? Are you going to be doing a lot more walking and standing on the job that might trigger that problem knee?

What Turns You On in Your Off-Hours?

Many employers subscribe to the theory that, "If you want something done, give it to a busy person." So, you want to portray yourself as an active, vital individual. Take this opportunity to paint a self-portrait of a well-rounded individual.

> ### 60. What do you like to do when you're not at work?

My advice is to talk about both active and passive activities, and be sure to emphasize those activities that may complement your on-the-job duties. For example, if you're applying for a position as a bookstore manager, mentioning that you read three books a week is highly appropriate.

101 Interview Questions

Shy away from the controversial. You may tend toward the conservative and be sitting across from the "last of the red-hot liberals." Do you really want your off-hours interests to come between you and the job you're after? And don't brag about interests that could cause a squeamish employer to envision a prolonged sick leave.

It's generally safe to talk about most sports activities—participating in team sports, coaching children and indulging in singular activities such as swimming, running, walking or bicycling. Avoid emphasizing activities that are likely to spark concern or controversy, such as sky diving or hunting.

As a rule, employers like activities that show you are community-minded and people-oriented. Your involvement with the Chamber of Commerce, Toastmasters, the Rotary Club, or fund raising for charities is likely to earn points. However, consider carefully mentioning any religious or political activities that may alienate the interviewer.

In short, be sure you *don't*:

1. **Sound like a couch potato.** "I'm a Giants fan. I never miss a game. I also catch every episode of 'Married With Children,' 'L.A. Law' and 'Love Connection.' And I tape my soap operas every afternoon, so I can catch up on them on the weekends."

2. **Seem headed for a collapse.** "I play racquetball, coach a softball team, am on the board of directors of the local museum, plan to run for city council this fall and, in my spare time, attend lectures on Egyptology at the university." (Whew! How will you find the time and energy for work?)

3. **Boast about dangerous activities.** "I like to challenge myself. Next weekend, I'm signed up for another bungee jump. I need something to keep me pumped up until rugby season starts."

4. **Bring up controversial interests that may be personally objectionable to the interviewer.** "I'm always on the front lines at Greenpeace demonstrations." Or, "My family is active in the Holy Roller Church."

Can We Talk?

As you relax in the spell of a skilled interviewer who has developed a knack for asking questions that are sure to get you talking, your guard will come down again. So don't be surprised if you field more questions, like these:

---

61. How would your co-workers describe you?

Of course, they would describe you as an easy-going person who is a good team player. After all, you've found that "a lot more can be accomplished when people gang up on a problem, rather than on each other."

Once again, the personal inventory you completed in Chapter 1 will come in handy. Cull words from the lists you've titled "My strongest skills," "My greatest areas of knowledge," "My greatest personality strengths," and "The things I do best"—and put them in the mouths of co-workers and friends.

62. How do you generally handle conflict?

I hope that you can honestly answer this question this way:

> *"I really don't get angry with other people very often. I'm usually able to work things out or anticipate problems before they occur. When conflicts can't be avoided, I don't back down. But I do try to be reasonable."*

Or,

> *"I've had confrontations with co-workers who weren't holding up their end of a job. I feel that employees owe it to their bosses, customers and co-workers to do their jobs properly."*

63. How do you behave when you're having a problem with a co-worker?

Now it's time to relate a specific incident, and talk about what you learned from it. For example:

> *"I had to work with a designer who was obstinate about listening to any of my suggestions. He would answer me in monosyllables and then drag his feet before doing anything I requested.*
>
> *"Finally I said, 'Look, we're both professionals. Neither of us has the right answer all the time. I notice that you don't really like my suggestions. But rather than resist implementing them, why don't we just discuss what you don't like, like adults?'*

"That worked like a charm. In fact, we actually became friends."

---

64. If you could change one thing about your personality with a snap of your fingers, what would it be? Why?

Choose a trait you've listed as a weakness that you don't allow to get in the way of your work. You might say:

"Boy, I had a hard time with procrastination in college. But I licked it because burning the midnight oil all through exam week every semester was driving me nuts. I have to confess, I still have the urge to procrastinate. (You might smile disingenuously here.) *I wish that I never felt like putting things off. But I know what will happen if I do."*

---

65. Describe your best friend and what he or she does for a living.

---

66. In what ways are you similar or dissimilar to your best friend?

Here are two more ways of saying, "So, tell me about yourself" now that your guard is all the way down. If the theory holds that best friends are very much alike, play to it. Take pains to describe a person that the company would find easy to hire.

Tips for Tooting Your Own Horn— Without Becoming a "Blow Hard"

- **Don't get carried away.** Only the most annoying people don't find it difficult to talk about themselves in a flattering way. And that's what you'll be doing on the interview— constantly tooting your own horn, until even you will want to change the tune.

  You'll be saying what a great person your friends think you are, what a pleasure your supervisors thought it was to have you on their team, that there are only a few little adjustments you'd like to make to your personality.

- **Stress the traits companies are looking for.** Enthusiasm, confidence, energy, dependability, honesty. Formulate answers that suggest these characteristics. Think about what you would want in an ideal employee if you owned a company. Wouldn't you want a problem-solver? A team player? Someone who is enthusiastic about working hard to achieve goals?

- **Be creative.** A friend of mine had to work his way through college. Rather than participate in low- or no-pay internship programs or extracurricular activities, he pumped gas and stocked supermarket shelves during the summer. These "menial" positions were in no way related to the career he was studying for—publishing. And to compound things, publishing is a very internship-oriented field. Many companies like to hire candidates who have spent their summers fetching coffee for editors and art directors.

My friend knew there would be searching questions about how he had spent his summer vacations from his Ivy League interviewer. So he was ready with this response:

"I wish I'd had more time to write for the school paper. Whenever I wasn't studying, I pretty much had to work to pay for college. But I learned a number of things from the jobs I held that most people learn only after they've been in their careers for a while—such as how to work with other people and how to manage my time effectively."

See what I mean? Now it's time to go on to the "Twilight Zone" of the interview. You're about to enter the realm of the hypothetical.

Chapter 9

What if Everyone Called in Sick, and...?

It's time to go to work, quite literally.

Through your answers to hypothetical questions, like the ones I've posed in this chapter, you'll be measured on how well you perform—before you step into the job! Do you have the resourcefulness, logic, creativity and ability to think under pressure? The interviewer hopes to find out by subjecting you to the *situational interview*.

After conjuring up a series of real or hypothetical situations, none of which you can realistically predict or specifically prepare for, the interviewer will watch you squirm—or sink.

Situational interview questions can come in any shape or style. I've given you only a handful of samples here. But once you get the idea, see if you can outsmart the interviewer. If you have a detailed description of the job you're applying for, use your imagination to try to anticipate a number of situations that might come up once you're behind the desk.

> **67. Say your supervisor left an assignment in your "in" box, then left town for a week. You can't reach him and you don't fully understand the assignment. What would you do?**

The interviewer is most likely looking to see whether you have an appropriate respect for hierarchy and deadline demands.

If there is truly no way to reach your boss or leave a message via voice mail or electronic mail, you'd suck up the courage to approach your boss's supervisor.

Of course, you would do this in a way that would not reflect badly on your boss by explaining that you and your boss simply missed the chance to discuss the assignment before he had to leave the office. Because you're not yet familiarity with the company's procedures, you simply want to be sure that you understand the assignment, so you can start on it as soon as possible.

> **68. The successful candidate for this position will be working with some highly trained individuals who have been with the company for a long time. How will you fit in with them?**

Your answer should indicate your eagerness—as the new kid on the block—to learn from your future co-workers. You don't want to raise any doubts about how they might react to you. So convey the fact that, while you are certainly bringing something to the party (skills, knowledge, your own insights), you realize you have a lot to learn from the people you'll be working with.

---

69. Your supervisor tells you to do something in a way you know is dead wrong. What would you do?

This is a tough question, so why not acknowledge it with an answer like this:

> *"In a situation like this, even the best employee runs the risk of seeming insubordinate. I would pose my alternative to my supervisor in the most deferential way possible. If he insisted that I was wrong, I guess I'd have to do it his way."*

---

70. How will you handle the least interesting or least pleasant tasks of this job?

An interviewer posing this question usually will build in specific aspects of the position, such as: "You won't always be looking for creative solutions to our clients' tax problems. Most of the time, you'll be churning out returns and making sure you comply with the latest laws. You're aware of that, of course?" You might answer:

> *"I'm sure that every job in the accounting field has its routine tasks. They have to be done, too. Doing those tasks is part of the satisfaction of*

doing the job well. They make the relatively infrequent chances we do have to be creative even more satisfying.

> **71. You've had little experience with budgeting (or sales or marketing, or whatever). How do you intend to learn what you need to know to perform well in this job?**

"Well, throughout my career, I've proven to be a quick study. For example, when my company's inventory system was computerized, I didn't have the time to go through the training. But the company that supplied the software had developed some computer-based tutorials and training manuals. I studied them and practiced at home. I hope that I'd be able to do something similar to pick up the rudiments of your budgeting system."

You could also mention other options, such as learning from professional publications and seminars. Show your initiative and resourcefulness in getting up to speed quickly. The interviewer wants to be sure you won't just be sitting around twiddling your thumbs and complaining that you don't know what to do next. Reassure him or her that you plan to do whatever it takes to go right on learning throughout your tenure.

What's the Worst that Could Happen?

Now, how would you step in and save the day? If you don't know as much as you'd like about the position you're interviewing for, spend some time with industry and trade publications. Focus on articles written to help people in this type of position solve common problems— or that suggest tips, tricks and tools designed to increase everyday efficiency.

You want to demonstrate that you're ready to step right in and handle a tough situation with a cool head.

For My Next Trick...

It's also a good idea to sharpen up your working knowledge and skills. Interviewers like to pose problems you can solve on the spot. These exercises are intended to demonstrate your proficiency in the areas most important to the job.

Preparation makes perfect. If you come up blank, or use a fact or formula inaccurately during one of these exercises, it will be difficult, if not impossible, to recoup your credibility. That would be especially unfortunate after you've gotten this far.

Caveat: Different companies may use slightly different terms for the same procedure or material. So explain your terminology up front to make sure you're communicating clearly.

How to Shine in Any Situational Interview

- **Admit that a tough situation would make you nervous.** You might even panic momentarily. No interviewer is looking for a candidate bent on plunging right in—and then flailing about without thinking of consequences or alternatives. Nervousness calls forth the adrenaline that often fuels creative strategies.

- **Take a moment to think before you answer.** This shows you are not likely to plunge into any situation with a hot-headed response. Rather, you are taking time to weigh the alternatives and choose the best course of action.

- **Avoid throwing the "bull."** No matter what the interview technique, quash the temptation to exaggerate or downright fabricate a response.

- **Show that you have a grasp of the real world.** Admit that you have a lot to learn about this company and the position. This approach is far more effective than trying to sell yourself as a savior.

- **Plan your answers to a number of different situations ahead of time.** Assume that some of these questions will be about areas of knowledge and skill you have yet to develop, so learn as much as you can about what you don't know. And have a strategy for finding the information or resources you currently lack.

Palms a bit sweaty? That's to be expected. But with preparation comes the promise of continued success as you clear each hurdle in the interview circuit.

Chapter 10

Getting Into the School of Hard Knocks

It's still true. The more work experience you have, the less anyone will care about what you did at Boola Boola U. Interviewers tend to care most about real-world, on-the-job experience.

But if you have precious little of that, this chapter was written for you. It is designed to guide the relatively inexperienced candidate facing that age-old Catch-22: you need experience to get the job, but how can you get experience if you can't get a job?

So it's back to "Creative Thinking 101."

You want to portray yourself as a well-rounded person while you were in school. If you weren't a member of many official school clubs or teams, talk about other activities you engaged in during college. Did you work part-time? Tutor other students? Work for **extra** course credit?

---

72. What extracurricular activities were you involved in? What made you choose those? Which of them did you most enjoy, and why?

Again, interviewers are looking for industrious people, not individuals who do just enough to eke by. So, this isn't a good place to joke, "Well, I didn't do much but drink beer on weekends, John,"—especially if it is true!

(There is never a particularly good time to joke during an interview. After all, one person's innocent joke is another's reason—unfair or not—to reject a candidate!)

---

73. What led you to select your major? Your minor?

---

74. Which of your courses did you like most/least?

If you were a liberal arts major, talk about the skills you developed in some of your courses: writing ability, debating and language skills. Assuming that you took courses related to the job at hand, focus only on those that are career-oriented.

Those courses you mention as your least favorite should be any that are not directly related to your eventual career. Try to develop answers that have to do with the subject, rather than the workload or the professor's personality. Talking about troubles with an authority figure will introduce a possible negative into your current candidacy. And complaining about too much work is not the best way to impress any prospective boss—especially these days, when staff cut-backs mean you'll probably be called upon to handle more work than your predecessors.

---

75. If you were to start college over again tomorrow, what are the courses you would take? Why?

Think about changes you would make in your course selections that would have produced a better candidate for this job. Should you have taken more marketing courses, an accounting course, a statistics seminar?

Don't say, for example, that you would have gone away to school so that you could date more. At the same time, don't be afraid to admit that it took you a little while to find the right course of study. Then talk about how valuable courses unrelated to your career were in your development.

---

76. What are your most memorable experiences from college?

Again, concentrate on experiences related to the job at hand. It might be very touching that you met your best friend for life in college, but it will hardly seem relevant to the interviewer.

Experience...Of a Sort

No company really believes that you're going to hit the ground running right out of college or graduate school. Training and experience will be necessary to make you productive. So, as a relatively inexperienced candidate, you can expect an interviewer to do a bit of probing—trying to determine how "trainable" you are.

---

77. What did you learn from internships (or why don't I see any) on your resume?

Stress how the real-world internship experience you've had complemented your academic training. But never pretend that college is where you learned the "Secret of Life." No interviewer is going to react favorably to someone who acts like he or she knows it all.

---

78. In what courses did you get your worst grades? Why? How do you think that will affect your performance on the job?

Many companies will ask to see copies of your college transcripts if you don't have work experience. So you might as well spill the beans now!

If you flunked every accounting course, you're probably not applying for an accounting job, right? So, hopefully, you can blame any bad grades you may have received in some of your electives on the amount of time and effort you were putting into your major.

Special Tips for Recent College Grads

- **Don't be afraid to say you'll need help.** And when you do, that you'll ask for it. Not many companies are looking for—or expect to find—a 22-year-old know-it-all.

- **Admit that you don't have all the answers.** Or begin a lot of your answers with "I think..." or "From what I know about the industry,..."

- **Don't appear squeamish at the idea of going through the school of hard knocks.** Many baby boomers think that baby busters— you and your friends—have severe attitude deficiencies. Tell the interviewer, "Sure, I know this position has its share of unpleasant duties, but I'm sure everyone who's had this job before me has learned a lot by doing them."

- **If it took a while for you to find your direction, admit it.** Nobody has all the answers at 18 or 19. How many people know from the start that they wanted to be accountants or hospital administrators? Most interviewers will not be surprised that you changed majors as an undergraduate. Show how your other studies contribute to making you the best candidate.

- **Don't answer any question about who paid for your educational expenses or about any outstanding educational loans you may be carrying.** Go ahead and play up

135

the fact that you received a full academic scholarship or were industrious enough to work your way through school, if you want to. But, by law, you don't have to say any more. For more detail on how to recognize and deflect illegal questions, see Chapter 12.

Chapter 11

There Are No Innocent Questions

I'll never forget this story a friend told me. As the head of recruiting for a rather large company, he spent weeks at a time interviewing scores of candidates for a wide variety of openings. With so much practice, he got to be a pro at knowing immediately when a candidate wouldn't work out—and "releasing" the unsuspecting person with a simple "Thanks for stopping by" before the interview even got underway!

Here's how it worked. On greeting a young woman applicant for a field sales position one morning, my friend asked, "How are you?" The applicant immediately began whining about the fact that it was raining and she had a run in her stocking.

This was a cue to my friend. He turned to her and, feigning embarrassment, said, "Oh! Are you here to apply for that field sales position? I'm sorry. We forgot to call. We filled the position yesterday. But we'll keep you in mind for other, similar positions that come along. Thanks for stopping by."

Watch What You Say

This story demonstrates an interview truism that few candidates realize: There is no such thing as an innocent question. You are being judged from the moment the interviewer sees you (or hears you on the telephone)—until the offer of employment is made.

There are many seemingly innocent questions that can do you in very quickly. Here are just a few:

> **79. How are you today?**

> **80. Did you have any trouble finding us?**

You are doing just fine, thank you. And no, you didn't have any trouble at all! That's because (don't admit to this; just do it) you took the time to get directions from the interviewer's assistant.

Again, it all comes down to being positive. I'm not suggesting that you plaster an idiot grin on your face and go on like a "Stepford" employee. But I do urge you to make every effort not to let anything negative (even the crummy weather!) enter into any part of your interaction with the interviewer.

Since my recruiter friend told me his little story, I know I pay much more attention to the answers candidates give to these little "throwaway" questions.

---

81. Do you know much about our company?

Believe it or not, many candidates think this is merely an ice-breaker, and simply answer "No."

Don't *you* follow suit! After all, why would you go into one of the most important encounters of your life so thoroughly unprepared? And then admit it?

I have urged (OK, nagged) you to do your homework. This is where your research will come in handy. Toss out a few salient (and positive) facts about the company, and finish by lobbing a question back into the interviewer's court. For example:

> *"Boy, what a growth story Starter Up is! Didn't I read recently that you've had seven straight years of double-digit growth? I read in your annual report that you're planning to introduce a new line of products in the near future. I jumped at the chance to apply here. Can you tell me a little bit about this division and the position you're interviewing for?"*

Is He Just Passing Time?

Over the years, I've taken to asking some out-of-the-blue questions of job candidates. And, according to what I read in human resources journals, I'm not at all out of the ordinary.

Many interviewers will try to lure you away from the "standard" interview questions. By now, these questions have become clichés. You've memorized the correct answers to each one, just as if you came into possession of a "stolen" exam. The real test is in how you answer those questions that come from out of the blue. For example:

---

82. What's the last book you read?

No doubt, advertisers ask this question of celebrities in those glossy profiles for Dewar's for the same reason an interviewer will ask the question of you. Because what someone chooses to read can say volumes about what kind of a person he or she is.

But before you reel off your reading list, consider this. Right or wrong, many interviewers seem to think that people who read nonfiction are more interested in the world about them than fiction readers, who they may believe are looking for an escape.

So, rather than talk about the latest thriller you couldn't put down, opt for a popular how-to book. This will demonstrate that you're interested in *Thriving on Chaos* or *Swimming with the Sharks* or, generally, trying to improve your knowledge and skill as a business person.

---

83. What's the last movie you saw?

Mention a popular, but noncontroversial movie. It won't do you a bit of good to gleefully admit it was "Friday the 13th, Part 86."

Do you want your taste in foreign films or left-wing documentaries to stand between you and a job? It's much better to stay with that goofy Tom Hanks movie. (If you insist your preferences shouldn't matter, feel free to discuss your ideas on "Blue Velvet.")

Tips on Avoiding a One-Minute Interview

- **No question is a throwaway.** The interview begins the moment you walk in the door (or pick up the telephone). So give careful consideration to all of your answers.
- **Exhibit the traits employers are looking for.** No matter what you're talking about, exude confidence, enthusiasm, energy and intelligence.
- **Answer carefully—and noncontroversially.** Why open up a can of worms? You may be inviting the interviewer to "go fishing."
- **Remember, this is still a job interview.** Not a meeting of the local literary society or movie fan club. An answer that helps you get the job is preferable to the one that accurately reflects your literary or cinematic tastes.

Now, on to some more less-than-innocent questions that also are less-than-legal.

Chapter 12

Are There Any *Wrong* Questions?

In an ideal world, companies and managers would judge every applicant solely on the basis of the skills and experience necessary to perform the job.

But it should come as no surprise that our world is far from ideal. In the real world, many managers and companies discriminate against people of color, people with disabilities, even women whom they may simply assume are planning to have children sometime during their future employment!

Few of us can claim to be completely objective when judging other people. But the fact is that you, as a candidate for any job, *do not have to answer* questions related to your race, nationality, marital or financial status—or even a disability, if it is unrelated to how well you are able to perform the job.

Illegal or "Inappropriate?"

If an interviewer is foolish enough to make an issue of your nationality, marital status or other personal information, should you leap out of your chair and make a citizen's arrest right there in the interview? No.

But you should sit up and take notice. Every state has regulations governing what may and may not be asked of an applicant during the pre-employment (application and interviewing) process. Just asking the wrong question is not illegal in itself. But it may open an employer up to a lawsuit, if an otherwise-qualified applicant is passed over for a job based on his her answer. Few companies are willing to take that chance. So when it comes to "inappropriate" questions, most employers tread lightly.

But regulations don't preclude the subtle techniques some interviewers use to get applicants to volunteer information. As an applicant, it's still up to you to dodge the bullet. The key is knowing when a question is inappropriate—and not surrendering any information that might come back and hurt you.

A Litmus Test for Interview Questions

Every question the interviewer asks you should pass this test: "Does it have to do with my job?"

Past that, it pays to check with your state's Fair Employment Practices Commission for a list of questions considered inappropriate for employers to ask on job applications and during pre-employment interviews.

In the meantime, here are some questions that should trigger alarms in your head during even the most "congenial" interview.

Questionable Queries

You can't stop an interviewer from drawing conclusions about your lineage from the color of your skin, eyes or hair during a personal meeting. But never surrender that information over the telephone—or hand over a photograph of yourself before you accept a job.

84. Is that an Irish (or Italian or Vietnamese or whatever) name?

Employers may not ask about your ancestry, descent, parentage or nationality—or that of your parents or spouse. It's OK to volunteer that you're proficient in a language other than English, but the interviewer cannot ask you how you learned to read, write or speak those languages.

Let's say your last name is "obviously" Italian. When you greet the interviewer, he remarks, "Rutigliano. That's Italian, isn't it?" What do you do? Just smile politely—and don't answer at all. It is quite possible that the interviewer meant absolutely no offense.

If the interviewer still doesn't get the hint and continues to allude to your Italian heritage, you might say, "I really don't see what my ancestry has to do with my application for this job." If you try to handle the situation diplomatically, you can stay on the interviewer's "good" side.

If an employer tries to pressure you into submitting a photograph of yourself to accompany your job application, simply say, "I don't have a suitable photograph available at this time. Of course, if I'm offered this job, I'd be happy to have one taken."

Only After You Have the Job...

The Federal Immigration Reform and Control Act of 1986 prohibits employers from hiring "aliens"—people who are not properly authorized to work in this country. *Once you have accepted the offer*, you will be required to document your right to work by surrendering one of the following:

- A United States passport.
- A "green" card.
- A combination of a birth certificate or social security card and a driver's license.

---

85. This is a Christian (or Jewish or Muslim or whatever) company. Do you think you would be happy working here?

This may be a sneaky way of finding out your religious affiliation. The interviewer may be looking for a reaction—"pro" or "con" that might influence his hiring decision.

Don't fall for it. Employers may tell you which religious holidays the company observes. But they cannot ask you for any specific information in this area.

If an interviewer presses you to reveal your affiliation, simply say:

"I like to keep my religious beliefs separate from my work, and I respect that right in the people I work with."

But if you find yourself dodging too many of these "bullets," maybe you should take a moment to think about whether you want to work for a supervisor who has shown himself to be ignorant and insensitive. If you don't care that he's an insensitive boob—you just want the job—then don't make an issue out of his comments. It's up to you.

Those Subtle "Stingers"

Often an interviewer's bias is not overt. Many interviewers use subtle ploys designed to get you to volunteer just the information that they may use to disqualify you from the running.

---

86. Are you a family man (or woman)?

You may be—and proud of it. But resist the temptation to whip out the latest pictures of your children. Why? After all, what could seem more innocent than chit-chatting about your fiancé, spouse or kids? What's the harm in letting an employer know about your tentative plan for having a child within a year?

Maybe there's no harm in it. But then again, you never know how an interviewer may interpret your answers. If you're planning to have a child within a year, for example, an interviewer may wonder whether you will begin to curtail your hours at work. If you're engaged to be married, he might assume that you'll be so wrapped up in wedding plans that your attention won't be focused on the job at hand.

Interviewers may not ask about your marital status or plans for marriage or for having children. If you already have children, you're not obliged to reveal their ages or the arrangements you've made for childcare. In many states, married women are not required to give an employer their maiden name—unless they've worked under another name at previous companies listed on their resume.

Karen's Slip

During her interview at one of the largest companies in the country, my friend Karen had little trouble deflecting the questions she knew to be inappropriate. But as the skilled interviewer continued to shift gears—moving back and forth between job-related questions and very personal issues—she let her guard down just once. She began an answer with "My husband..."

The interviewer pounced on her "slip"—asking questions about Karen's husband. What did he do for a living? How did he feel about his wife having a job? The interviewer wanted more insight into the role Karen's career played in her family life, so she tried every ploy she knew to get the information from Karen.

Meeting Halfway

Rather than simply refusing to answer a question—and creating bad feelings between you and the interviewer—you may find it helpful to confront what you believe might be the employer's concerns about your situation. For example, if the interviewer keeps digging for information about whether you have children, or plan to, he may be concerned about your commitment to the job. You might respond by saying something like:

"I sense that you are concerned about my ability to be here on a regular basis to put in the work necessary to meet deadlines. Just let me assure you that I have always been a reliable worker who's committed to getting the job done well and on time. In fact, in my last position, I was never late to work once and I consistently completed all projects ahead of deadline."

See? Without answering any questions about children or family plans, you addressed the real issue—the employer's concern about your commitment to your job.

87. What is your birth date?

Age can be a loaded issue for many employers. If you're in your late 40s or 50s, some employers may worry about your energy flagging or your health failing. Don't give them ammunition in the form of a number.

Employers cannot ask for your birth date or about facts that might reveal your age, such as the year you graduated from high school. Interviewers may only state that hiring is subject to verification of legal minimum age requirements and that employees under the age of 18 must provide a work permit.

But age, like race, can be easy to guess. So again, take a positive tack. Play up the benefits of your experience and assure the employer that you have all the vitality for work you had when you were in your 20s. You might say:

"The more I've accomplished, the more effective I've become. When I was just starting out I was so full of energy I was like a loose cannon. Now I find I can accomplish more in less time because I know where to find the resources I need and how to work effectively with all kinds of people."

88. Do you belong to any organizations?

Think carefully about your answer to this question. An employer can ask about (and should only be interested in) your membership in organizations, professional societies or other associations considered important to your performance on the job.

It's a good idea to leave out the names of any organizations that might provide "clues" to your race, religious creed, color, national origin, ancestry, sex or disability.

None of Your Business!

Employers do not have the right to ask anything that is not directly related to your ability to perform the job at hand. That includes questions about your general physical health or economic wealth.

89. Do you have any physical disabilities?

Interviewers may only ask about a physical or mental disability that will directly affect your performance on the job.

Your general physical health is not fair game, although you may be asked to take a physical examination after you receive an offer. The outcome of this examination must be related to essential functions of the job—so the employer has the right to condition the offer on the results.

Employers may *not* ask about whether you have:

- An existing mental condition.
- Received workers' compensation.
- Problems with alcohol or drugs.
- HIV, AIDS or AIDS-related syndrome.

A Word About AIDS

This is an area of increasing concern for employers. Although new laws and regulations will likely be written, currently HIV infection, AIDS and AIDS-related medical conditions are considered "disabilities" under the Federal Americans with Disabilities Act.

If you test positive for HIV or AIDS (or any other disability) in a pre-employment medical examination, the employer cannot use that information as ground for withdrawing the offer—unless the extent of the illness substantially inhibits your ability to do the job or poses a reasonable threat to the safety of others in the work place.

90. What's your economic status?

A prospective employer may only ask what you're currently earning.

Your current or past assets, liabilities or credit rating are not fair game. This includes whether you own a home or any information about a past bankruptcy or garnishment of wages (except when permitted by federal and state laws governing credit-related information). Again, it's wise to consult specific guidelines in your state.

What's Your Record?

A dishonorable discharge from the military or an arrest that did not result in a conviction does not mean your professional life is over. In the majority of cases, these facts should remain in your past.

Be aware, however, that regulations do differ from state to state and from industry to industry. For example, under the Federal Deposit Insurance Act, banks are prohibited from hiring individuals convicted of any crime involving dishonesty or breach of trust, even if the conviction is more than seven years old.

91. Have you ever served in the military?

If you have and want to bring to light the skills and knowledge you gained from that experience that are relevant to the job you're applying for, go ahead. But be aware that you're *not* required to give the dates of your military service or the type of discharge you received.

92. Have you ever been arrested?

Unless you're applying for a position as a police officer or with the Department of Justice, a prospective employer is not entitled to know whether you've been arrested—unless the arrest resulted in a conviction.

In some states, employers may only ask about felonies, not misdemeanors. If you have a record, do some research.

When Asked the Wrong Question

Despite a plethora of lawsuits charging employers with discriminatory hiring practices over the past 25 years, inappropriate questions still are commonly asked during interviews. This is particularly true of interviews by hiring managers, who may not be up on legal issues. If you're asked an inappropriate question, you have three choices:

1. You can be a constitutionalist and refuse, on principle, to answer—even if you'd come up smelling like a rose if you did.
2. You can be a pragmatist and provide answers you feel wouldn't hurt you, while you tactfully side-step questions you think could hurt you.
3. You can be a little of both.

Beware the Wily Interviewer

Most interviewers who are trying to get at information that is considered inappropriate won't be obvious. Here's a case of subtle discrimination.

After making it through three interviews for a job at one of the big tobacco companies, a friend of mine thought she was "in." But during her final interview, the interviewer offered her a cigarette. She replied, "No, thanks. I don't smoke."—without realizing that she had inadvertently said "no" to the job as well!

Notice the subtlety. The interviewer never asked, "Are you a smoker?" or "Do you smoke?" Turning down an applicant because she refused to engage in an unhealthy activity might put the company on questionable legal and public relations ground. But by getting her to volunteer the information, the interviewer had what he needed to disqualify her from the running.

(When I heard this story, I couldn't help but wish she had answered, "No, thanks. I don't smoke during interviews." Perfectly true—and nearly as coy as the interviewer's gambit!)

What to Do After the Fact

If an interviewer has asked you questions not related to the job on offer, and you believe you weren't hired based on your refusal to answer or the information you did provide, you might have grounds for charging the employer with discrimination.

The operative word here is "might." The burden of proof is on you. You will have to prove that the questions were asked for the purpose of discriminating among applicants. For example, if the manager asking all those questions about Italian ancestry subsequently hired another Italian, you wouldn't have much of a claim, despite the fact that you were asked inappropriate questions.

If you do think that you have grounds for a charge of discrimination, you should file your charges simultaneously with the appropriate state agency and the federal government's Equal Employment Opportunity Commission (EEOC). The EEOC generally will wait until the state agency has conducted an investigation, then conduct an investigation of its own.

As you might expect, the wheels of government agencies can creak at their own slow pace. In fact, you might not hear anything for years! Even then, an agency will only determine whether there is reason to believe your charge is true. Therefore, if you are anxious for justice, you should request that the EEOC issue you a notice 180 days after you file your charge.

If You're In the Right

If the EEOC determines that your complaint is valid, it will first attempt to mediate the dispute between you and the employer. If an agreement can't be reached, the Commission will either file its own suit or issue you a letter giving you the right to sue the employer. You must file your suit within 90 days of receiving such a letter.

Say that you win your lawsuit. Don't expect to receive one of those colossal jury awards that seem to occur weekly on television's "L.A. Law." The most you'll probably get from the employer is the equivalent of a year's salary.

Tips for Fending Off Illegal Questions

- **Know your rights.** Do some research to find out what questions are out of bounds in your particular state, industry or profession.

- **Don't open the door for the interviewer.** That is, don't bring up subjects you don't want to talk about. If you do, the interviewer is likely to ask what would otherwise have been illegal questions—if you hadn't opened the door first.

- **Change the subject.** If you feel that the interviewer is asking you questions that shouldn't be asked, the first step is to try to shrug them off and change the direction of the conversation.

- **Give the benefit of the doubt.** After all, you are here because you want the job. So it's up to you to weigh your personal reactions to certain searching questions against your desire to have this job. Many hiring managers may not realize they are in the wrong. Give them the benefit of the doubt.

- **Warn the interviewer—subtlely.** Tell the interviewer in a non-threatening way that you know the questions he or she is asking are inappropriate. This should deliver the message that you know your rights and aren't willing to be a victim of discrimination.

- **End the interview.** If the interviewer refuses to back off, end the interview quickly. After all, would you really want to work at a company or for a person capable of such narrow-minded attitudes? If you think you have a strong case, look into bringing formal charges against the company and the interviewer.

One Last Word...

None of the information or advice in this chapter should be taken as legal advice. I am not an attorney. If you feel a prospective employer is guilty of discrimination, your first step should be to contact the appropriate government agencies, as well as an attorney to accurately assess your rights and options under federal law as well as the laws and regulations in your state and industry.

Chapter 13

Wrapping Things Up

OK, you've made it this far, you *must* have the job by now. Anyway, there's absolutely no way to screw it up at this point, right?

Don't be so quick to relax. The closing questions of an interview should be handled with care. In short, there are still likely to be some tough questions ahead. Here goes.

It's Your Turn to Speak Up

Yes, you've been holding your own—fielding every question volleyed your way with skill and grace. But now it's time for the interviewer to turn the tables.

> **93. Do you have any questions?**

Never, I repeat, never answer with a "no." How can you make one of the most important decisions of your life—whether to work for this company at this job—without knowing more?

Even if you think you're sold on the position or you're clear on the responsibilities, you must speak up here. If you don't, the interviewer will assume you are uninterested. And that can be the kiss of death to you as an applicant, even at this late stage.

What Do You Want to Know?

While it's easy to get caught up in the challenge of impressing the interviewer with your brilliant answers, it's also important that you don't lose sight of the fact that you also have a goal. You are trying to determine whether this situation is right for you—whether this job is worthy of your talents and commitment.

With this in mind, arm yourself with the following list of questions.

> *"Can you give me a formal, written description of the position? I'm interested in reviewing in detail the major activities involved, and what results are expected."*

This is a good question to pose to the screening interviewer. It will help you prepare to face the hiring manager. If a written description doesn't exist, ask the interviewer to dictate as complete a description of the job to you as possible.

> *"Does this job usually lead to other positions at the company? Which ones?"*

You don't want to find yourself in a dead-end job. So find out how you can expect to advance after you land this job. What happened to the person you would be replacing? Is he or she still with the company?

Try to pursue this line of questioning without coming across as if you can't wait to get out of a job you don't even have yet! If you ask in a completely nonthreatening manner, your ambition will be understood—and even welcomed.

> *"Tell me some of the particular skills or attributes that you want in the candidate for this position?"*

The interviewer's answer should tell you how much your traits are valued. With this information, you can underline those traits you possess at the close of the interview to end it on a strong note.

> *"Please tell me a little bit about the people with whom I'll be working most closely."*

I wish someone had told me about this question before my last job interview! The answer can tell you so many things. For example: How good the people you are working with are at their jobs and how much you are likely to learn from them. Most importantly, you'll find out whether the hiring manager seems enthusiastic about his or her team.

A hiring manager usually tries to put on his or her best face on during an interview, just as you do as the prospective candidate. But catching the interviewer off guard with this question can give you a glimpse of the real expression behind the "game face."

If he or she doesn't seem enthusiastic, you probably won't enjoy being part of the team. This particular hiring manager may attribute little success, and perhaps a lot of headaches, to the people who work for him or her.

101 Interview Questions

"What do you like best about this company? Why?"

This might seem like something you shouldn't ask under any circumstances. If the boss hems and haws a lot over this one, it may indicate that she doesn't really like the company that much at all.

If she's instantly enthusiastic, her answer should help sell you on her and the company.

The answer to this question can give you a good sense of the values of the organization and the hiring manager. If she talks about nothing but products and how well her stock options are doing, it indicates a lack of enthusiasm for the people-side of the business.

"What is the company's ranking within the industry? Does this position represent a change from where it was a few years ago?"

You should already have some indication of the answer to this question from your initial research, particularly if the company is publicly owned. If you have some of this information, go ahead and build it into your question:

"I've read that the company has risen from fifth to second in market share in just the past three years. What are the key reasons for this dramatic success?"

Here are some more:

"What new products is the company considering introducing over the next year or two?"

"Has the organization had any layoffs or reductions in its work force over the past couple of

years? Are any others anticipated? How was this department affected?"

"Will the company be entering any new markets during the next few years? Which ones?"

"You say you are anticipating a growth rate of 'x' percent over the next few years. Will this be accomplished internally or through acquisitions?"

Do shy away from asking about days off, vacation, holidays, sick pay, personal days, and so on. You'll seem like someone who is looking for a chance to get out of the office before you even start!

Details, Details

94. Are you willing to travel?

Yes, of course you are. Your family understands the demands of your career and is supportive when you need to spend some time away from home. Does that mean you want to be away three weeks out of four? Probably not. Unless you are unwilling to travel at all, don't let this question cost you the job. (If the job requires far more travel than you are prepared for, what are you doing on the interview?)

95. Are you willing to relocate?

If you really are, say so. "Absolutely. In fact, I would look forward to the chance to live elsewhere and experience a different lifestyle and meet new people."

If you're not, say so. "Well, not unless the job is so terrific that it would be worth uprooting my family and leaving my relatives and friends. Does this position require a move? I'm obviously very interested in it, so I might consider relocating."

96. May I contact your current employer?

Why do people ask this question? You probably will feel like saying, "Sure, after you give me this job and I don't have to worry about getting canned because I've been out looking for another job."

But you'll sound better saying: "Sure you can—after we come to an agreement. I think it's best if they hear about this from me first."

97. May I contact your references?

Of course. Tell the interviewer that you will get back to him or her with a list of references that afternoon or, if it is already afternoon, the very next day.

Does this stalling make you seem unprepared? Shouldn't you go into the interview with the list ready to hand over to the interviewer?

Frankly, in the world of interviews, stalling for a little time before giving references is SOP (standard operating procedure). The reason you want to wait is so you can tell your prospective references that a call might be coming from Mr. Krueger of Trikadeka-phophia, Inc. If your references are indeed going to say wonderful things about you, they should be prepared to do so.

Caveat: Employers are growing more reluctant to provide references because of a rise in the number of claims of defamation and misrepresentation. Because job references are partially privileged communications, it's a good idea to try to get an inside line on what is being said about you to a prospective employer. As an applicant you may be able to approach a current or former employer to work out a narrative job reference that is accurate and amenable to both of you. With your consent and involvement, former employers may be more willing to discuss your strengths and weaknesses and the circumstances surrounding your departure in a positive light.

98. Is there anything else about you I should know?

You might not think you have anything else left to say—but you'd better have! This is your chance—on a silver platter—to close the sale. You'd be a fool to walk away from it.

Develop a short answer to this question, one that plays upon your strengths, accomplishments, skills, and areas of knowledge. For example:

"Mr. Krueger, I think we've covered everything. But I want to re-emphasize the key strengths that I would bring to this position.

- *Experience. The job I'm currently in is quite similar to this one, and I would be excited by the chance to apply what I've learned at WidgetLand working for your company.*

- *Management skills.* I run a department almost equal in size to this one. I'm a fair and effective supervisor.

- *A record of success.* I've won two prestigious industry awards. I would bring that creativity here.

- *Enthusiasm.* I am very excited about the prospect of working with you here at Trikadekaphobia. When do you expect to make a decision?"

This type of answer should underline the points that you have been trying to make throughout the entire interview. By ending with a question, you ask Mr. Krueger to take some action. This is an effective selling technique that should give you a good indication of your chances of getting the job.

Keys to Wrapping Up a Successful Interview

- **Be prepared to ask questions**. Remember, an interview is a two-way street. Your job is to find out if the company, the industry, and the hiring manager are right for you. Don't be shy about asking the interviewer some rather tough questions.

- **Don't ask about time off.** At least not before you're offered the job.

- **Don't ask about salary or benefits.** Wait until you are offered the job. You don't want money to be a factor when the interviewer is considering whether you are the best person for the job.

- **Prepare a closing argument.** This should briefly summarize your strengths, skills and accomplishments, and underline those that the interviewer has already told you are key to the job.

- **Don't give out the names of your references.** Instead take time to prepare these people that they may hear from your prospective employer and let them know what you want them to stress (or leave out).

Over and Out?

You may be feeling as though you've just gone 14 rounds with Mike Tyson. Weary, but elated. Assuming you're the winning candidate what more could there be? Well, there's just one more little jab before the final bell. In the next chapter, we'll talk about negotiating salary and benefits.

Chapter 14

Money Talks

No one likes to talk about money during an interview. It seems "indelicate," somehow. But that doesn't mean you should avoid it completely. Just remember that timing is everything.

My own rule of thumb is simple. Don't discuss dollars and cents until after you've convinced the interviewer that you're the best person for the job.

That's why I've relegated the first question on salary to number 99. Until you've made it over the first 98 interview hurdles, the interviewer is still assessing your ability. And he or she is probably still seeing other contenders as well—some whose talent comes cheaper than yours.

But even if an interviewer tries to pressure you into naming a specific number early in the game, avoid committing yourself. Instead, name a very broad range. You might say, "I believe a fair wage for this kind of position would be something like $30,000 to $40,000." Be sure the bottom end of that range is no less than the minimum salary you would be willing to accept for the position.

Once the employer has made his decision, you're in a much stronger bargaining position.

---

99. What sort of salary are you looking for?

First you must have a pretty good idea of what your particular market will bear. If you don't know the high and low end in your area (city and state) and industry, do some research. Make sure you know whether these figures represent just dollars, or a compensation "package" that may include insurance, retirement programs and other value-added benefits.

If you're a woman, make sure you know what men are making doing the same job. You're bound to find a discrepancy. But you should request and expect to earn an equivalent salary, regardless of what women predecessors may have earned.

I'm Worth It!

Even more important to these negotiations is your confidence in your own worth. By this time, you've worked hard to sell the interviewer on your value as a future employee. Just remind him of what he's already decided.

Harry is a friend of mine who is not only eminently qualified, but also a heck of a good interview, and he knows it.

So, when a recruiter called Harry with a job lead that sounded perfect for him—but paid only $40,000—Harry told her: "I want that job. Send me on the interview. After they've met me, they'll be willing to pay me what I want."

It sounds cocky, but Harry knew what he was doing. During the interview process, he studiously avoided the subject of salary. When the interviewer finally asked, "What would it take to get you over here?" Harry showed his cards.

"I understand the job has a top salary of $40,000," he said. When the interviewer affirmed that, he went on: "Well, I would need more than that. I came here because the job sounded terrific. In fact, the job description Gretchen gave me, and which you've just elaborated on, has my name written all over it."

To make a long story short, Harry got the salary he wanted because he had already sold himself. If he had asked for the same money earlier in the interview, he probably would have been out of the running.

What if your initial offer isn't accepted? It's time to negotiate.

---

100. The salary you're asking for is near the top of the range for the job. Why should we pay you this much?

Remind the employer of the cost savings and other benefits he'll enjoy when you come on board. Pull out your specifics again, if necessary. For example, you might say:

> *"I was able to cut my previous employer's expenses by 10 percent by negotiating better deals with vendors. I think it's reasonable to expect that any additional salary we agree to would be offset by savings I could bring the company."*

You've come to an agreement, and the last piece of business before you start your new job.

---

101. When can you start?

If you've been laid off or fired, you can start immediately, of course.

But if you're still working for someone else, you must give at least two week's notice to your current employer—more if you are leaving a position in which you had considerable responsibility.

As eager as you may be to get started on this new job, I know I don't have to remind you that it's never wise to burn bridges. You never know when you might have to cross one of them again! So be as accommodating as you can. You might offer to help your current employer find and train your replacement, for example.

If it will be several weeks before you can assume your new responsibilities full-time, offer to begin studying literature or files in your off-hours. Or come in to the office in the evening or on a weekend to meet members of the staff and begin to familiarize yourself with the lay of the land. You might even be called on to attend a company event or seminar.

Tips on Wrapping Up a Winning "Package"

- **Wait until you receive an offer.** Defer any question of salary that comes up early in the interview with an answer like this: "Colleen in human resources indicated the salary range for this position, and it seems about right to me."

  Or, "I'd like to know a little bit more about the job responsibilities and the level of expertise you're expecting before I can feel comfortable about suggesting a salary."

- **Know your worth.** Remember that the company wants you. They have decided you are the best candidate they have met. This puts you in a position of power. If they balk at your initial salary demand, remind them of a few specific benefits they stand to gain from hiring you.

- **Research compensation levels.** Look within your industry and locally—within your city and state. If you don't already know the salary range for the specific position you're considering, find out. You need to go to salary negotiations armed with this information.

- **Negotiate the perks.** Make sure you understand the value of all the potential benefits in the salary/benefits package. Benefits can vary widely. Some companies buy employees company cars and club memberships. Others give bonuses or extra time off.

171

- **Go for the top.** If that is more than the company will pay, the interviewer will counter with another offer. Work toward a compromise from there.
- **Get it in writing.** Especially if you negotiate a complex, nonstandard salary benefits package. Be sure you have something in writing—either a letter or memo from the employer, or one you've sent that's been accepted—before you give notice to your current employer.

Did We Cover All the Bases?

That would be impossible. But we have covered a lot of ground. I can promise you that some interviewers will come up with humdingers that you won't see in these 101—some even I couldn't imagine.

How will you handle them? If you have developed your personal inventory, practiced answers to the most common questions you should expect to be asked, developed a list of questions to ask the interviewer and done all your homework about the company—you'll answer them very well indeed.

I've asked you to put in a fair amount of work throughout this book. But the result should be well worth the effort. Trends show that you're likely to be "out there" interviewing many more times during your career than other generations of professional people. The better you get at it, the more of an edge you'll have in shaping a successful and rewarding career.

If you didn't receive an offer this time, keep plugging. I'll leave you with some tips on after-interview etiquette in the next chapter. And, of course, my best wishes for your career success.

Chapter 15

After-interview Etiquette

Once you step out from under the bright lights and shake hands with the interviewer, it will probably take all the composure you can muster not to kick up your heels and run out of the office.

But in your hurry, don't forget that the process is not quite over. Whether you're waiting by the phone for word or off to your next "ordeal," there are a few standard rules of etiquette you should follow.

- **Ask when the hiring decision will be made.** If you don't get word by that time, it's perfectly acceptable to call the employer to inquire about the status of the position.
- **Write a thank-you note.** Make it short and sweet. Begin by thanking the interviewer for taking the time to meet with you. Then restate your interest in the company and the position and find a way to remind the interviewer of how you can use your skill and experience to address one of the key requirements of the job.

Type it in business-style and be sure there are no typographical or spelling errors.

Here's a good example:

Dear Mr. Jones,

Thank you for taking the time to discuss the position of purchasing manager with me yesterday. It was a pleasure meeting you and learning more about Start Up, Co.

During our meeting, you mentioned that you'll be shopping around for a new computerized materials management system soon. During my years at Consolidated, Inc., I reviewed and worked with a number of these systems and I have a few thoughts about which ones might work best for you. I'd be happy to share my thoughts with you at any time.

Again, thank you for your consideration. I look forward to hearing from you and the possibility of joining your staff.

Sincerely,

Jane Anderson

Jane Anderson

Remember that if you met with more than one interviewer, you should send thank-you letters to each individual you talked to.

Finishing Touches

- **Nourish your network.** If a colleague or former associate referred you to the company or arranged a personal introduction with the interviewer or hiring manager, be sure to drop that person a note of thanks as well.
- **Replay the highs—and the lows.** What went well during the interviewing process? What could you have done better? The point is not to berate yourself for what you did or didn't say. You merely want to make sure you keep doing the things that worked—and working on what didn't—so you can ace your next interview.
- **Rewrite your resume.** Did the interviewer have any questions about information that you could clarify on your resume? Did you find yourself talking about accomplishments you forgot to include? If so, now is the time to revise your resume—before you send it out again.
- **Keep in touch.** The hiring process can move at a snail's pace in corporate America. Often, the larger the corporation, the slower the pace. So don't panic if a week or two passes before you hear anything. No news may be good news. If time stretches on, it's OK to call to find out if the job has been filled. Use the opportunity to

remind the employer of your interest and qualifications.

- **Accept—in your own time and on your own terms.** Never accept an offer at the time it is tendered. Take a day or two to think about it. Tell the interviewer when you will announce your decision. If you do decide to refuse the offer, politely tell the employer why you don't feel you can accept the position.

- **Congratulate yourself.** You made it through one of life's more stressful experiences with flying colors. You've proven you're a real pro. Now you're on your way.

Chapter 16

The 101 Toughest Interview Questions

Chapter 5: Work—And the *Real* You

Chapter 6: What Are You Doing Here?

Chapter 7: OK, Off With Your Defenses

Chapter 8: Let's Get Personal

Chapter 9: What if Everyone Called in Sick, and ...?

Chapter 10: Getting Into the School of Hard Knocks

Chapter 11: There Are No Innocent Questions

Chapter 12: Are There Any Wrong Questions?

Chapter 13: Wrapping Things Up

Chapter 14: Money Talks

Index

101 Great Answers to the Toughest Interview Questions

101 Interview Questions

101 Interview Questions

101 Interview Questions